Meister Eckhart, from Whom God Hid Nothing

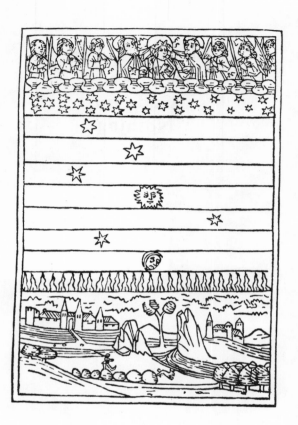

MEISTER ECKHART

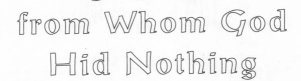

from Whom God Hid Nothing

Sermons, Writings, and Sayings

Edited by
DAVID O'NEAL

Foreword by
BROTHER DAVID STEINDL-RAST, O.S.B.

Shambhala
Boston & London
1996

For my mother, Darlene O'Neal

Shambhala Publications, Inc.
Horticultural Hall
300 Massachusetts Avenue
Boston, Massachusetts 02115

9   8   7   6   5   4   3   2   1

First Edition
Printed in Canada
⊗ This edition is printed on acid-free paper that meets
the American National Standards Institute Z39.48 Standard.
Distributed in the United States by Random House, Inc.,
and in Canada by Random House of Canada Ltd

Library of Congress Cataloging-in-Publication Data

Eckhart, Meister, d. 1327.
[Selections. English. 1996]
Meister Eckhart, from whom God hid nothing: sermons, writings,
and sayings / edited by David O'Neal; foreword by David Steindl-Rast.
p.   cm.
Includes bibliographical references.
ISBN 1-57062-139-X (alk. paper)
1. Mysticism—Catholic Church—Miscellanea.   2. Spiritual life—
Catholic Church—Miscellanea.   3. Catholic Church—Doctrines—
Miscellanea.   I. O'Neal, David, 1954–   .   II. Title.
BV5080.E3213   1996   95-22647
248.2′2—dc20   CIP

Contents

Contents

Foreword: On Reading Eckhart

His Holiness the Fourteenth Dalai Lama feels quite at home in the world of Meister Eckhart, and His Holiness Pope John Paul II quotes the same Meister Eckhart on occasion in a sermon. Now, there's a bridge builder between traditions! Should this come as a surprise? No, it shouldn't surprise us, for Meister Eckhart is a mystic. The mystics of all traditions speak one and the same language, the language of religious experience.

When I use the term *religious experience,* I mean something that is not at all the private domain of those whom history has called "the mystics" in a special sense; rather, I mean something familiar to you and me and to everyone likely to read this book. Religious experience is simply our awareness of communion with the Ultimate. (Meister Eckhart calls the Ultimate "God," but those who feel less comfortable with that word are certainly not barred for that reason from experiencing the reality to which the word *God* points.)

Communion with the Ultimate may surprise and overwhelm us unawares in peak moments of aliveness—on horseback, on a mountaintop, on the prow of a ship, under the dome of the night sky, or in a lover's arms. Or it may happen that we experience the same communion with the Ultimate as slowly, slowly dawning on us during a long-drawn-out struggle to remain faithful to ourselves, during a painful process of grieving, or during seemingly endless nights at the bedside of a dying friend. What counts is that it happens, not how. What counts is that we somehow experience a limitless belonging to that unspeakable mystery which alone ultimately matters.

For some, this experience lasts barely longer than the glimpse of a falling star, seen and forgotten; forgotten, or suppressed among a thousand preoccupations with other matters. "We had the experience, but missed the meaning," as T. S. Eliot puts it. For a moment we touched a live spark, but we did not fan it into fire, we let it go out. Not so those whom we call the great mystics. They spend their lives on what all of us, in our best moments, long for. The poet Rilke expresses this longing in a glowing prayer (as translated by Steven Mitchell):

> O shooting star
> that fell into my eyes and through
>   my body—:
> Not to forget you. To endure.

The flash of religious experience challenges us to three all-demanding tasks: embodiment, remembrance, endurance. Those brave ones who rise to this challenge endure the blinding vision, remember it in whatever they do, and so embody vision in action. By this process, mysticism becomes a way of life. It may even become the starting point for a religious tradition.

All the different religions can be traced back to an experience of communion with the Ultimate by their founders or reformers. Historic circumstances lead then to the great diversity of religious traditions. Yet all those diversities are only so many expressions of one and the same mystical core—expressions of the sense of ultimate belonging. This mystical core needs to bring forth so many different myths and teachings, needs to be celebrated in so many different rituals, because it is inexhaustible.

Not only is the mystical core of religion inexhaustible, it is also ultimately unspeakable. The heart of all ritual is stillness; the heart of all teaching is silence. The mystics of every tradition know this and keep telling us that "those who speak do not know, and those who know do not speak." Yet those same mystics write volumes and volumes. Meister Eckhart is no exception. The language of mystics, however, explodes ordinary language. What is left, after that, is silence, a silence that unites.

Language is meant to build bridges. Yet how often language divides. It divides when we get stuck in concepts and abstractions, alienated from experience. It is a dreadful thing when this happens to religious language, yet it tends to happen in every tradition. This is why we need the language of mystics to blow to pieces the conceptual walls that divide us—long enough for us to get in touch again with that silent ground of our unity in experience. Once we are grounded in silence, conceptual thinking, too, will regain its proper function. No longer will concepts be the bars of a mental prison, but rather the bars of a musical score—for a music of silence.

Never before in history was it more urgent for all of us to learn the language of the mystics than in our time, when division threatens to destroy us. The mystics of every tradition speak a language that unites. Think of Rumi, of Mirabai, of Kabir, of Black Elk. Or in the Christian tradition, Hildegard, Teresa, John of the Cross, and our Meister Eckhart. No wonder their readership is continually expanding. More and more people realize that the writings of mystics are an urgently needed medicine for our time. Yet reading them is not always an easy task. And Meister Eckhart is for some of us the most difficult one to read.

Let me admit my own difficulties with Meister Eckhart. Quite likely the moment you hear his name some favorite quotation comes to your mind. "The eye with which I see God is the very eye with which God sees me," is one of my own favorites. I'd venture the guess that Meister Eckhart is a hundred times more often quoted than read. Those who make the effort to read him find two kinds of books: collections of short quotations and editions of longer texts. That is where my trouble starts. Whenever I browse through quotations, I want to see them in their wider context, but when I start digging through longer passages, I find that one needs to move a lot of soil before hitting one of those precious nuggets.

At his best, Meister Eckhart deliberately appeals to the reader's own experience. "Though I put more faith in the scriptures than in myself," he writes, "it is easier and better for you to learn by means of arguments that can be verified." Whenever he follows this plan, he speaks to me; experience speaks to experience, heart speaks to heart. But soon I find myself in the midst of the most arid scholastic abstractions and am reminded of the time after a forest fire had laid waste the woods around our monastery. I trudge through lifeless stretches, highlighter in hand, until I hit again upon a patch of fresh green, a spot where a spring of mystic experience bubbles out. This book whets our appetite by a section of short quotations and then offers us larger excerpts of Meister Eckhart's writings. I do recommend to its readers to highlight their favorite sayings.

All right, I do it myself. Pen in hand, I start reading and I underline the sentence "Man's best chance of finding God is to look in the place where he left him." That's not just deep, it's marked by the fine humor typical of some of the best spiritual insights. But what of the translation? As far as I know, Meister Eckhart consistently uses *homo* in his Latin works and *Mensch* in his German ones. Neither is correctly translated by "man." Both terms include women. If "human being" sounds clumsy in English, at least it doesn't foist sexist language on Meister Eckhart. Matthew Fox does better on this score, but translation is always a problem.

"Poetry," it has been said, "is that which gets lost in translation." There is too much truth in this statement, especially when we remember that poetic language comes closest to communicating mystic insight. Meister Eckhart's most poetic passages are at the same time his most alive, his most lifegiving ones. But I have more serious problems with his writings, problems which the best translation will not be able to remedy. Let me give two examples. I take the first from a passage about unity, the second from a treatise on detachment.

Delightedly I highlight the passage "to know the truth one has to dwell in unity and be the unity." Another passage nearby sheds light on the first and vice versa. God is one. "Be one, that thou mayest find God." I highlight that too. But suddenly it strikes me: these two memorable passages about wholeness spring from the author's mystical experience, yet they stand in a speculative context that gives the lie to that wholeness. It is a section marked by blatant dualism that distorts the biblical tradition on which it is based. Saint Paul sets "the spirit" (true aliveness) over against "the flesh" (all that is opposite to life, all that is death-bound). Here, however, the opposition becomes one between spirit (more in the sense of "mind") and "body," between "the inner" and "the outer." Not only this, but the outer is "evil" and has strong feminine overtones, while the good inner half of this dichotomy is clearly masculine. What shall I say? I remind myself that we are all children of our time and share its blind spots. We have no right to receive the wisdom of a teacher unless we are ready to offer compassion in turn.

Meister Eckhart himself offers us passages that glow with compassion. Here is one: "Do you think you do not have God simply because you have no devotion? If you suffer from this, then just this will be your devotion." Great wisdom and compassion of a shepherd of souls is contained in these lines. And that is what Meister Eckhart was, for most of his life, a guide of souls. This saintly teacher who spoke so eloquently of "the laughter of God" did not live in an ivory tower. Day by day he was laboring to heal the suffering of his time and the suffering of souls entrusted to him. When I think of him as this compassionate teacher, I find it easier to read his less inspired passages with compassion, to wait patiently until the sometimes arid scholastic gives me another lush mystical message.

Nowhere is it more difficult to disentangle Meister Eckhart's mystic insight from wrongheaded speculations than when he writes about detachment. "No one is more cheerful than the one who lives in the greatest detachment." Clearly this was written by the mystic who had heard the living God laughing. When he put on his philosopher's cap, however, he was apt to lose touch with the biblical God and mistake the stillness of love for the Unmoved Mover. The Incarnation and Passion of the eternal Word "affected the immovable detachment of God as little as if He had never become man." Or: "As God, having no motives" (not even love?), "acts without them, so the just man acts without motives." That's where the application gets outright dangerous: "The just man has no reason for doing what he does." This sentence expresses the ultimate freedom of one who is totally at the disposal of God's Holy Spirit. But it can too easily be misused by any harebrained space cadet who quite definitely "has no reason for doing what he does." All I can offer is a warning.

"We are the cause of all our obstacles," Meister Eckhart writes. He must have realized that this was true of himself whenever he attempted to know God speculatively instead of "seeing" God with the eyes of his heart. When he was at his best, he knew this: "There are some who think felicity consists in knowing God. But I would not subscribe to this." (Not in his better moments, at least.) "The first condition of bliss is the vision of God face to face."

And again he writes: "All those who want to make statements about God are wrong, for they fail to say anything about him. Those who want to say nothing about him are right, for no word can express

God." Here the mystic is speaking, and suddenly we recognize a voice that unites: in the depth of the Christian tradition, this is the Noble Silence of the Buddha.

It is this common ground shared by the two traditions that many readers will find most engaging. This, then, is how I'd suggest you approach this book: armed with a pen for highlighting lines that speak to your heart; armed also with that rarely-talked-about virtue, compassion for the teacher. And keep your inner ears attuned to that silence which comes to word without being broken. It is the sure mark of the mountain region from which the two great rivers of Buddhist and Christian tradition spring forth and flow out.

Even when Meister Eckhart writes as a Christian about suffering—the topic where we should least expect common ground with Buddhism—he finds this common ground with sleepwalking sureness, as long as it is the mystic in him who speaks. Take this, for instance: "Our Lord says in the Psalms of a good man that he is with him in his suffering." *With* him! This is not the God above the clouds, enthroned in immovable detachment. This is a lover who suffers when we suffer. I ponder this mystery, and a word of the Dalai Lama comes to my mind; it shall stand at the end of this foreword, since his name stands at its beginning.

"Your Holiness," someone asked, "your Buddhist tradition has so wonderful a way of overcoming suffering. What do you have to say to the Christian tradition that seems to be preoccupied with pain?" With his compassionate smile the Dalai Lama gave an answer that went straight to the common ground of the two traditions. "Suffering," he said, "is not overcome by leaving pain behind. Suffering is overcome by bearing pain for the sake of others." (Christ and Bodhisattva embraced at that moment. Across seven hundred years of history I could hear Meister Eckhart laughing with joy. Or was it God's eternal laughter?)

BROTHER DAVID STEINDL-RAST, O.S.B.
Big Sur, California
Summer Solstice 1995

Editor's Introduction

Meister Eckhart represents, according to Ananda K. Coomaraswamy, "the spiritual being of Europe at its highest tension."* The modern impulse to understand that tension as the confrontation between a free thinker and an oppressive religious establishment falls away upon reading Eckhart's writing: the conflict with the Church that came up late in his life is not found there. Yet there is an unmistakable tension to be found in Eckhart, and we feel it today, even when we read him completely outside his medieval Catholic context: it is the tension between philosophic concepts and the inexpressible, between words and silence, between human and Divine. Eckhart inhabited that place where words became impossible, yet he dared to speak, and did so eloquently, honestly, and compassionately. More than seven hundred years later we are amazed by Meister Eckhart; the words inspire trust; we feel we know him. Yet he seems to disappear under the scant known details of his life.

His given name may have been John. He was born in Germany, in a village called Hochheim, Thuringia,

---

*A. K. Coomaraswamy, *The Transformation of Nature in Art* (Cambridge: Harvard University Press, 1934), p. 61.

not long before 1260, and he entered the order of the Dominican friars at Erfurt while probably still quite a young man. He was sent by the Dominican order to the University of Paris sometime before 1280, then to the order's institute at Cologne to study theology, and finally again to Paris to complete his master's degree, around 1294. The academic title Meister is the name by which he has ever since come to be known.

By 1300 he was back in Germany and installed as "Prior of Erfurt, Vicar of Thuringia." It is in this period that some of his talks were recorded and circulated under the weighty title *These Are the Talks of Instruction That the Vicar of Thuringia, the Prior of Erfurt, Brother Eckhart of the Preaching Order Held for Such of His Spiritual Children as They Asked Him about Various Things as They Sat Together in Evening Table-Conversation*. In English translation this collection has most commonly been called "Table Talk" or "Talks of Instruction."

In 1303 Eckhart was made Provincial of the Dominican order over a province that included nearly all of middle and lower Germany and which contained sixty religious communities, both men's and women's. In 1307 he was made Vicar of Bohemia as well. This period coincides with the rise of his enormous popularity as a preacher. In 1312 he became head of the Dominican order at Strasbourg. By 1320 he was Prior of Frankfurt. From the Frankfurt period comes "The Book of Divine Consolation," written for the bereaved Queen of Hungary, in which he spells out his principal ideas on the relationship between the human and the divine, and the treatise "On Detachment."

Eckhart's popularity brought his writing under the scrutiny of Church authorities and ultimately resulted in his being brought to ecclesiastical trial in 1325. (The details of the trial and the theological arguments that led to his condemnation can be read about in Blakney's *Meister Eckhart*.)★ Though the date of his death is unknown, his excommunication on 27 March 1329 was posthumous.

His writings remained popular and influential. A number of sayings and fragments came to be attributed to him. His recorded sermons circulated widely, and the title assigned by an anonymous scribe to one of the most famous of them—"This Is Meister Eckhart from Whom God Hid Nothing"—has become an enduring epithet. Eckhart's influence is clear on the lives and works of his successors Johannes Tauler,

---

★Raymond B. Blakney, trans., *Meister Eckhart: A Modern Translation* (New York: Harper & Row, 1941).

Henry Suso, John Ruysbroek, and the Brotherhood of the Friends of God, and on an entire generation of Rhineland mystics. His later admirers have included figures as diverse as Hegel and Matthew Fox, and his writings strike sympathetic chords today with people from a range of spiritual traditions—from Christians in search of roots to Buddhists who find in Eckhart the common ground betwen Buddhism and theistic systems.

The central purpose in all of Eckhart's work becomes clear after only a small amount of reading. It has been succinctly expressed by the Eckhart translator and scholar Raymond B. Blakney:

> It could be said that Meister Eckhart was a man of one idea—one very great idea, to whom nothing else mattered much. That idea was the unity of the divine and the human. . . . No one ever expressed more decisively than he the immeasurable difference between the Creator and the creature, between God and man. Creatures, of themselves, he was never tired of saying, are nothings.
>
> Still, in spite of their endless differences, if God and man are of the same genus, it must be possible to set free the divine kernel of being in man's inmost self by the ever-increasing conquest of his outer self-identity. This divine ker-

nel, this "little spark" of God which is concealed within the shell of selfhood, is as high above all that is purely human and personal as heaven is high above earth. It is the germ of eternal life and the seed of God, the point of divine grace from which man may derive his worth and hope. (*Meister Eckhart,* pp. xx–xxi)

This book consists of selections from among several modern English translations of Eckhart: by Raymond B. Blakney, James M. Clark, Hilda Graf, and John V. Skinner. It also includes material adapted from the first widely available English translations by C. B. de Evans and Franz Pfeiffer, with minor changes made to modernize usage and punctuation for clarity. Beginning with short fragments and sayings attributed to Eckhart, then moving on to the longer treatises and sermons, it is intended to provide a taste of Meister Eckhart's teaching on the inestimably important "little spark" of the Divine in each person, as a starting point for further exploration.

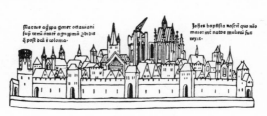

Sayings

1

What is truth? Truth is something so noble that if God could turn aside from it, I could keep to the truth and let God go.

2

Meister Eckhart said that no person in this life may reach the point at which he can be excused from outward service. Even if he is given to a life of contemplation, still he cannot refrain from going out and taking an active part in life. Even as a person who has nothing at all may still be generous for his will to give, another may have great wealth and not be generous because he gives nothing; so no man may have virtues without using them as time and occasion require. Thus, those who are given to the life of contemplation and avoid activities deceive themselves and are on the wrong track. I say that the contemplative person should indeed avoid even the thought of deeds to be done during the period of his contemplation but afterwards he should get busy, for no one can or should engage in contemplation all the time, for active life is to be a respite from contemplation.

3

Meister Eckhart asked why people are so reluctant to seek God in earnest. Then he made this comment: When one is looking for something and sees no sign that it is where he is searching, he will keep on looking there only with painful reluctance. If, however, he begins to find traces of it, then he will hunt gladly, gaily, and in earnest. The man who wants fire is cheered by feeling warmth and then joyously looks for the blaze. It is like that with people who ought to be seeking God: if they get no taste of the divine sweetness, they drag; but if a man lies in wait until he does catch the taste of the divine, ever afterward he is a glad seeker of God.

4

Earth cannot get away from heaven: let the earth drop downward or rise upward, heaven still penetrates it, imbuing it with strength and making it fruitful, whether it will or no. That is how God treats man: when he thinks to escape God, he runs into God's bosom, for every hideout is open to him. God begets his Son in you whether you like it or not, whether you sleep or wake—still God is at work. That man is not aware of it is the fault of his [spiritual] tongue, which is smeared with the scum of creatures, in which there is none of the salt of God's love. If we had God's love in us, we could taste God in all his works and we would accept anything as from God and finish his work along with him. In sameness [of intent] we are his only begotten Son.

5

Meister Eckhart, the preacher, also said this: There never was a struggle or a battle which required greater valor than that in which a man forgets or denies himself.

6

I have often said that a person who wishes to begin a good life should be like a man who draws a circle. Let him get the center in the right place and keep it so and the circumference will be good. In other words, let a man first learn to fix his heart on God and then his good deeds will have virtue; but if a man's heart is unsteady, even the great things he does will be of small advantage.

7

Some people want to see God with their eyes as they see a cow and to love him as they love their cow— they love their cow for the milk and cheese and profit it makes them. This is how it is with people who love God for the sake of outward wealth or inward comfort. They do not rightly love God when they love him for their own advantage. Indeed, I tell you the truth, any object you have on your mind, however good, will be a barrier between you and the inmost truth.

8

The just man loves God for nothing, neither for this nor for that, and if God gave him wisdom or anything else he had to give, except himself, the just man would not look at it, nor would it be to his taste; for he wants nothing, seeks nothing, and has no reason for doing anything. As God, having no motives, acts without them, so the just man acts without motives. As life lives on for its own sake, needing no reason for being, so the just man has no reason for doing what he does.

9

Meister Eckhart says: He who is always alone is worthy of God, and to him who is always at home is God present, and in him who stands always in the present does God the Father bear his Son unceasingly.

10

Meister Eckhart said: I never ask God to give himself to me, I beg him to purify, to empty me. If I am empty, God of his very nature is obliged to give himself to me to fill me.

How to be pure? By steadfast longing for the one

good, God. How to acquire this longing? By self-denial and dislike of creatures. Self-knowledge is the way, for creatures are all nothing, they come to nothing with lamentation and bitterness.

God being in himself pure good can dwell nowhere except in the pure soul. He overflows into her. Whole, he flows into her. What does emptiness mean? It means a turning from creatures: the heart uplifted to the perfect good so that creatures are no comfort, nor is there any need of them except in that God, the perfect good, is to be grasped in them. The clear eye tolerates the mote no more than does the pure soul anything that clouds, that comes between. Creatures, as she enjoys them, are all pure, for she enjoys creatures in God and God in creatures. She is so clear she sees through herself; nor is God far to seek: she finds him in herself when in her natural purity she flows into the supernatural pure Godhead, where she is in God and God in her, and what she does, she does in God and God does it in her.

11

Meister Eckhart, being questioned as to God's greatest gift to him, answered: There are three. First, cessation of carnal desires and pleasures. Second, divine light enlightens me in everything I do. Third, daily I grow and am renewed in virtue, grace, and happiness.

12

On one occasion Brother Eckhart said: There are five things that in whoever has them are a sure sign that he will never lapse from God. First, though most grievous things befall this man from God or creature, never a murmur does he make—no word but praise and thanks is ever heard. Second, at the most trying times he never says one word in his excuse. Third, this man desires of God what God will freely give and nothing else; he leaves it all to him. Fourth, nothing in heaven or earth can ruffle him; so settled is his calm that heaven and earth in topsy-turveydom would leave him quite content in God. Fifth, nothing in heaven or earth can cheer him, for having reached the point where nothing in heaven or earth can sadden him, so neither can it gladden him, except as trifles can.

A man as remote and far from his own self as the chief angel of the Seraphim is from him would have that angel for his own, as he is God's and God is his. And that is the bare truth, as God is God.

Saint Paul says: "The whole world is the cross to me and I the cross to you."

13

Brother Eckhart preached saying: Saint Peter said, "We have left all things." Saint James said, "We have given up all things." Saint John said, "We have nothing left." Whereupon Brother Eckhart asks: When do we leave all things? When we leave everything conceivable, everything expressible, everything audible, everything visible—then and then only we give up all things. When in this sense we give up all, we become flooded with light, exceedingly bright with God.

14

According to Meister Eckhart, God is not only the Father of all good things but he is the mother of all things as well. He is father, for he is the cause of all things and their creator. He is the mother of all things as well, for when creatures have gotten their being from him he still stays with creatures to keep them in being. If God did not remain with creatures after they had started their own life, they would most speedily fall out of being. Falling from God means falling from being into nothingness. It is not so with other causes; they can with safety quit the things they cause when these things have gotten being of their own. When the house exists its builder can depart, for it is not the builder alone that makes the house; the materials of it he draws from nature. But God provides the creature with the whole of what it is, with form as well as matter, so he is bound to stay with it, or it will promptly drop out of existence.

15

The soul is no different from Christ, except in that it has a born nature and a created nature. Christ does not have this in his eternal person. If the soul shed her born nature and her created nature, she would be all the same, just essence itself. I say, put off your creature; it is easy to shed the creature, for this is a labor of love and the greater the pain the greater the joy.

16

Whoever has three things is beloved of God: The first is riddance of possessions; the second, of friends; and the third is riddance of self.

17

God will never give himself openly to the soul . . . unless she brings her husband, that is to say, her whole free will.

From Table Talk

The Most Powerful Prayer of All and the Highest Work of All

～ ～

The most powerful prayer, one well nigh omnipotent, and the worthiest work of all is the outcome of a quiet mind. The quieter the mind, the more powerful, the worthier, the deeper, the more telling and more perfect the prayer is. To the quiet mind all things are possible. What is a quiet mind? A quiet mind is one which nothing weighs on, nothing worries, which, free from ties and from all self-seeking, is wholly merged into the will of God and dead to its own. Such a one can do no deed, however small, that is not clothed with something of God's power and authority. It behooves us to pray hard so that all our mortal members with their powers—eyes, ears, heart, mouth, and all their senses—are turned in that direction, and we must never stop until we find ourselves on the point of union with him we have in mind and are praying to, namely God.

Solitude and God-Getting

I was asked this question: Some people shun all company and like to be alone; their peace depends upon it. Would they not be better in the bosom of the Church? I said no, and you shall see why. The righteous man is righteous still in any place and any company, and the unrighteous man is unrighteous still in every place and in all company. The righteous man truly has God in him. But one who truly has God will have him in all places, in the streets and in the world no less than in the church, in the desert or the cell. If he has gotten him indeed and gotten him alone, he is proof against all hindrance. Why? Because having gotten God alone, he is ever bearing God alone in mind, is pregnant with God in all his acts as well as in all places, and all his works are being done by God. . . .

So if we give our whole mind to God, then it is he in fact who is doing all our works, and nothing whatever can disturb him, not company or place. Nor can anyone disturb the man who minds nothing, seeks nothing, relishes nothing but God, for God is united with this man in all his thoughts, and as God is not disturbed by any multiplicity, so nothing can disturb or diversify this man who is one in *the One* where all multiplicity is one and homogeneous.

Man ought to lay hold of God in everything, and he should train his mind to have God ever present in his thoughts, his intentions and affections. Watch your attitude toward God. When you are in church or cell, preserve that same frame of mind and take it out into the world, into its turmoil and its fitfulness. And, as I often say, speaking of equability, this does not mean putting all actions on a par—nor all places nor all people. That would be quite wrong, for praying is a better act than spinning, and church is a better place than the street. What it does mean is being even-tempered in your dealings, having unfaltering faith, and bringing to God an unwavering devotion. Being in this sense equable, no one, I warrant, could come between you and your God. But anyone for whom God is not really within like this, who must always go and fetch him from outside, from this or that, seeking him in changing modes, perhaps in work or in places or people, that person is easily distracted, for he has neither gotten God nor is not seeking him alone nor does not want nor mind him only and therefore he is hindered not merely by bad company but also good, not merely by the streets but by the churches, not by foul words and deeds alone but by

17

fair as well. The hindrance is in him because in him things have not all turned into God, for if they had, all would be well and good with him in every place and in all company. He would have gotten God whom no one can take from him.

Wherein does this true divine possession lie, this real God-getting? This real God-getting is a mental process, an inner turning of the mind and will toward God, not in one fixed and definite idea. It would be impossible for nature to hold it in the mind—or at least extremely difficult—nor is this the best way. We ought not to have or let ourselves be satisfied with any thought of God. When the thought goes, our God goes with it. No, what we want is a real (subsistent) God who far transcends the thoughts of men and creatures. This God does not disappear unless we turn our back on him of our own accord. He who has God thus, in reality, has gotten God divinely; to him God is apparent in all things. Everything smacks to him of God; everywhere God's image stares him in the face. God is gleaming in him all the time. In him there is riddance and return; the vision of his God is ever present to his mind. Like a man with a mighty thirst, he may be doing things other than drinking and thinking other thoughts, but whatever he is doing or whoever he is with or whatever sort of temper he is in, no matter what he is working at or thinking, as long as the thirst lasts, the idea of drinking will never leave him, and as his thirst increases, the stronger, more deep-seated, more present, more persistent the notion of drinking will grow. Or again, the ardent lover, wrapped up in some object and with no heart for other things, cares for that thing alone, not a jot for anything else. Well, wherever that man is and with whomever he is, whatever he is doing or undertakes to do, the idea of his beloved never fades from his mind. He finds it everywhere, and as his love grows stronger it haunts him more and more. Even so, this man will not be seeking rest, for no unrest disturbs him. He finds more favor in God's eyes if he takes everything to be divine, higher than the thing is in itself. I grant you this needs effort, application, careful cultivation of the interior life, and good sound sense and understanding of where to keep the mind in things and with people. This is not learned by flight, nor is it learned by one who runs away from things, who turns his back upon the world and flees into the desert. One must learn to find the solitude within wherever or with whomever he may be. He must discover how to enter things and, seizing God therein, get a clear impression firmly rooted in his mind, just as one learns to write. In order to acquire this art, a man must practice hard and often, however dull and troublesome it is and however much beyond him it may seem to be. With industry and patience he will get the knack. True, at first he will have to pay attention to each letter and impress it firmly in his mind, but later on, when he has mastered it, he will pay no attention to these hieroglyphics but will write freely, completely untrammeled by them. Whether it is penmanship or cunning to which he puts his art, it is enough to know that he is going to use it. Though he pays only little attention to his task and thinks of something else, still he goes on doing it in virtue of his cunning. And so this man in virtue of God's presence goes on shining without effort. What is more, he is alive to one pure nature in all things while completely unoccupied with the things themselves. This in its early stages is a matter of attention and forming definite impressions, as it is with the scholar and his art. Finally, the mind of man pervaded with a sense of God and throughly informed with the form of God and accustomed to him is able to see him without trying.

Unremitting Effort in the Highest Progress

No work is ever so properly begun or so well done, no man is ever so free and so certain in his actions, that he can afford to let his mind relax or go to sleep; but he ought with his twin powers, intellect and will, to be forever hoisting himself up and seizing, at the summit, his very best therein and guarding himself against evils of all kinds, subjective and objective; thus he never misses anything but is always making first-rate progress.

What to Do on Missing God Who Is in Hiding

It must be understood that goodwill misses nothing of God, but the mind is sometimes lacking in perception and is very apt to imagine that God has passed it by. Then what is to be done? Exactly the same as you would do if you were in the greatest comfort. Learn not to vary in the depths of woe but to behave in every way the same. Man's best chance of finding God is to look in the place where he left him. As it was with you when you last had him, let it be now while you have lost him—then you shall find him. Goodwill never loses, never misses God at any time. People often say, "We have goodwill." Theirs is not God's will, though; they want to have their own way and dictate to God to do so and so. That is not goodwill. We must find out from God what his will is. Broadly speaking, what God wills is that we should give up willing. Saint Paul's friendly conversation with our Lord, who spoke freely with him, availed him nothing till he surrendered his own will and said, "Lord, what wilt thou that I do?" Our Lord well knew what he had to do. So, too, when the angel appeared before our Lady: nothing she had so far done or said would ever have made her the Mother of God, but the moment she gave up her will, she became the true mother of the eternal God's Word: suddenly she conceived God. He was her natural son. There is no making of a proper man without surrender of the will. In fact, unless we give up our will without reserve, we cannot work with God at all. But suppose it came about that we did give up our own will altogether and had the heart to rid ourselves of every single thing inside and out for God, then we would have accomplished everything, and not before. Of such people few are to be found. Knowingly or unknowingly they want something definite, some experience of higher things. They are set on this condition or that boon. It is nothing whatever but self-will. Abandon to God altogether your self and all things without any qualms as to what he will do with his own. There are thousands of people dead and gone to heaven who never really gave up their own wills. There is no true and perfect will until, entering wholly into God's will, a man has no will of his own. The more this is the case with him, the more and the more safely he is established in God. One *Ave Maria* said thus with self-forgetfulness is better than a thousand said without; better one step in this way than a journey overseas in any other.

One who has quite done like this with everything of his is so safe in God that in order to get to him we must reckon with God first, for he is right in God with God all around him, as my cowl is around my head, and any person laying hands on me will first come in contact with my habit. Likewise when I drink, the drink has first to pass my tongue. There the drink is tasted. If my tongue is coated with bitterness, then however sweet the wine is in itself, it will be sour to me. The fact is that a man, once he escapes for good from his possessions, is surrounded with God, and creatures cannot touch him without first encountering God, and anything must go by way of God to reach him, and in doing so, it gets a flavor of him and becomes divine.

Why God Often Lets Good People, People Who Are Really Good, Be Prevented from Doing Their Good Works

The good God often lets his friends fall sick so that every prop they lean on or might cling to may give way. Loving souls find so much joy in doing many and great feats in the way of vigils, fasts, and so forth, or other things uncommonly fine and difficult, that it gives them intense pleasure and support and hope. In work they find help, refuge, and firm foothold, and it is precisely this that our God would knock away so that he himself may be their only prop and stay, and he does it out of kindness and compassion, for God wants nothing for his works except his own goodness. Our acts in no way help to make God give or do to us anything whatever. It is this idea our Lord would have his friends get rid of, so he undermines their faith in it to make them trust in him alone who intends to bestow kindness on them not for any reason but for love, that he may be their comfort and their stay and that they, finding that they themselves are really nothing, may admire in all the great gifts of God. For the more void and passive the mind that falls on God and is upheld by him, the deeper the man is gotten into God and the more receptive is he to the precious gifts of God. Man must build on God alone.

From The Book of Divine Consolation

First of all, one should know that the wise man and Wisdom, the true man and Truth, the just man and Justice, the good man and Goodness, are related to each other and are proportioned to one another as follows: Goodness is neither created nor made nor born; but it is giving birth and brings forth the good man, and the good man, in as far as he is good, is unmade and uncreated, and is yet the child and son of Goodness. Goodness gives birth to itself and to all it is in the good man: being, knowledge, love, and operation—it pours it altogether into the good man, and the good man receives all his being, knowledge, love and operation from the heart and inmost part of Goodness and from it alone. The good man and Goodness are nothing but one goodness, completely one in all things, except for the giving birth and the being born, and yet the giving birth of Goodness and the being born is in the good man altogether one being, one life. All that belongs to the good man he receives from Goodness in Goodness. There he exists and lives and dwells. There he knows himself and all that he knows, there he loves all that he loves and operates with Goodness in Goodness, and Goodness with him and in him all its works, according as it is written and the Son says: "The Father abiding in me doeth his works." "The Father worketh even until now and I work." All that is the Father's is mine, and all that is mine and of mine is my Father's: his in giving and mine in receiving.

One should know further that if we speak of the "Good," the name or word signifies and includes nothing else, no less and no more, than goodness pure and simple; nevertheless, we then mean the good in so far as it gives itself. If we speak of the "good man" we mean by this that his goodness is given, infused, and inborn in him from the unborn Goodness. Therefore the Gospel says, "As the Father hath life in himself, even so gave he to the Son also to have life in himself." He says: in himself, not of himself, for the Father has given it to him.

All that I have now said of the good man and of Goodness is equally true of the true man and Truth, of the just man and Justice, and of the wise man and Wisdom, of the Son of God and God the Father, of all that is created, that is not God, in which there is no image save the pure, sheer God alone. For thus says Saint John in his Gospel, that to all those he gave power to become sons of God, who were born "not of blood, nor of the will of the flesh, nor of the will of man, but solely of God."

By "blood" he means all in man that is not subject to man's will. By "the will of the flesh" he means all that is, indeed, subject in man to his will, yet with aversion and revolt, inclining to the desires of the flesh and belonging to soul and body together and which is not actually to be found only in the soul; and consequently the powers of the soul grow tired, weak and old. By the "will of man," Saint John means the highest powers of the soul whose nature and working is not mixed with the flesh and which are in the purity of the soul, separated from time and space and from all that still has some interest or pleasure in time and space. These powers have nothing in common with anything, in them man is modeled on God, of the race of God and of the family of God. And yet, since they are not God himself and are created in the soul and with the soul, they must be de-formed of themselves and transformed into God alone and be born in God and from God, so that God alone should be their Father, for thus they are also sons of God and God's only son. For I am the son of all that forms me and gives birth to me as equal to and in itself. In so far as such a man, son of God, good as the son of Goodness, just as the son of Justice, is solely its [i.e. of justice] son, it is giving birth without being born, and the son to whom it has given birth has the same being as Justice has and is and enters into the possession of all that belongs to Justice and Truth.

31

All this teaching that is written in the holy gospel and is known with certainty in the natural light of the reasonable soul, gives man true consolation for all his suffering.

Saint Augustine says: For God nothing is far or long. If you want nothing to be far or long for you, unite yourself to God, for there are a thousand years as the day that is today. In the same way I say: In God there is neither sorrow nor suffering nor tribulation. If you would be free from all tribulation and suffering, attach and turn yourself purely and wholly to God. To be sure, all suffering arises only from the fact that you do not turn solely toward and into God. If you were only formed and born in justice, indeed, nothing could cause you suffering, as little as justice God himself. . . . Therefore man shall take much care to detach himself from himself and from all creatures, and to know no father save God alone. Thus nothing can make him suffer or feel sorrow, neither God nor creatures, neither created nor uncreated things, and his whole being, life, knowledge, understanding, and loving is from God and in God and God.

There is something else that should comfort a man. If he is ill and his body is in great pain, yet having his home and all he needs of food and drink, medical advice and the service of his domestics, the sympathy and assistance of his friends: how should he then behave? What do the poor, who have the same or even greater illness and misery to bear and have no one to give them even cold water? They must beg their dry bread from house to house, in rain, snow, and cold. If you therefore want to be comforted, forget those who are better off and always think of those who are in a worse state.

I say further: All suffering comes from love and affection. If I then suffer because of transitory things, I and my heart have still love and affection for transitory things and I do not cherish God with all my heart and I do not yet love what God wants to be loved by me and with him. How, then, is it surprising that God should allow me rightly to suffer pain and sorrow?

Saint Augustine says: "Lord, I did not want to love you, but I wanted in my greed to possess the creatures with you; and therefore I lost you, for it is repugnant to you that one should possess the falsity and deceit of the creatures together with you, who are the Truth." He also says elsewhere that he is too greedy to whom God does not suffice. And again, in another place: "How could a man be satisfied by God's gifts in the creatures who is not satisfied by

God himself?" A good man should not find comfort but pain in all that is alien and different from God and not wholly God himself.

Now I will speak of something else. He cannot be a good man who does not will what God wills in every particular case, for it is impossible that God should will anything but good; and precisely in and through that God wills it, it is necessarily good and even the best. And therefore our Lord taught the apostles and us in them to pray every day that God's will should be done. And yet, if God's will comes to pass, we complain.

Seneca, a pagan master, asks: What is the best comfort in suffering and tribulation? And he answers: It is this, that a man should take all things as if he had desired and asked for them. For if you had known that all things happen from, with, and in the will of God, you would indeed have wished for them. A pagan master says: Prince and supreme Father and Master of the high heavens, I am ready for all you will; give me the will to will according to your will.

A good man should trust God in this, believe him and be certain and know him to be so good that it is impossible for God and his goodness and love to permit that any suffering or sorrow should happen to a man, except that he wants to spare man a greater sorrow or the better to console him even on earth or to bring a greater good out of it from which God's honor would appear better and more strikingly. However that may be, for the sole reason that it is God's will that this should happen, the will of the good man ought to be so completely one and united with God's will that man wills the same as God, even though it be to his own detriment, indeed his damnation. Therefore Saint Paul desired to be separated from God for God's sake and for the sake of God's will and God's honor.

A man should also think in his suffering that God speaks the truth and makes promises in his own name as being the Truth. If God forsook his word, his truth, he would forsake his godhead and would not be God, for he is his word, his truth. Now his word is that our sorrow shall be turned into joy. Surely, if I knew for certain that all my stones should be changed into gold, the more and the larger stones I had, the better I should be pleased.

Another, similar example: No container can hold two kinds of liquid. If it is to hold wine, we must necessarily pour out the water; it must become empty and void. If, therefore, you are to receive divine joy and God, you must necessarily pour out the creatures. The more perfect and pure the powers of the soul, the more perfectly and fully they take in what they grasp, and the more they receive, the greater joy they will feel, the more they will become one with what they take in, so much so that the highest power of the soul which is stripped of all things and has nothing in common with anything, will receive no less than God himself in the breadth and fullness of his being. And the masters say that no other joy and delight can be compared with this union and this bursting forth and this delight. Therefore, our Lord says so remarkably: "Blessed are the poor in spirit." Poor is he who has nothing. "Poor in spirit" means: as the eye is poor and devoid of color but receptive of all colors, so he who is poor in spirit is receptive of all spirit. Now God is the Spirit of spirits. The fruit of the spirit is love, joy, and peace. To be stripped, poor, to have nothing, to be empty—this transforms nature; the void causes water to climb mountains and performs many other marvels of which we would not now speak.

If, therefore, you want to have and find full joy and consolation in God, see to it that you are stripped of all creatures, of all consolation from creatures. For certainly, as long as creatures comfort and are able to comfort you, you will never find true comfort. But if nothing can comfort you save God, truly God will console you, and with him and in him all that is delight. If you are consoled by what is not God, you will have comfort neither here nor there. If, however, creatures do not console you and you do not enjoy them, you will find comfort both here and there.

Another consolation that might comfort a man: Supposing someone has for many years had honor and well-being and that now, by God's design, he loses it. Then a man should take wise thought and thank God. When he realizes the present harm and misfortune, he will appreciate how much advantage and security he had before, and he shall thank God for the well-being he enjoyed for so many years without appreciating how well off he was, and he should not be angry. He should realize that according to the natural truth [namely of his being] man has nothing but malice and infirmities. All that is good and goodness God has lent, not given, to him. He who recognizes the truth knows that God, the heavenly Father, gives all that is good to the Son and the Holy Spirit; to the creature, however, he does not give any good but only lends it. . . . Therefore I say: Since all that is good or consoling or temporal is given to man as a loan, what has he to complain of when he, who has lent it, will take it back? He ought to thank God that he has lent it to him for so long. He also should thank him that he does not take away altogether what he has lent him; indeed, it would only be just if God took back all he had lent him if man is angry that God takes back part of that which never belonged to him, of which he never was the master. Therefore Jeremiah the prophet rightly said when he was in great suffering and lamentation: "Many are God's mercies that we are not altogether destroyed." If someone has lent me his garment, his fur, and his coat, and took back his coat but left me his garment and fur in the frost, I should rightly thank him and be glad. And one should realize particularly that I am very wrong to be angry and to complain if I lose something; for if I want that the good I have should be given to me and not lent, I want to be master and want to be God's son by nature and perfectly, whereas I am not yet [even] God's son by grace.

One should also know that in nature the impression and influence of the highest and supreme nature is more blissful and delightful for every being than its own nature and essence. According to its own nature, water flows down into the valley, and this is according to its being. But under the impression and influence of the moon above in the sky, it denies and forgets its own nature and flows upward to the heights, and this flowing out is much easier for it than the downward flow. By this a man shall know whether he is as he should be; that it should be delight and joy for him to abandon his natural will and to renounce himself and wholly to go out from himself in all that God wills a man to suffer. . . . If therefore our Lord says: "He who will come to me, let him deny himself and take up his cross and follow me," this is not only a commandment as one normally says and thinks; it is a promise and a divine teaching, showing man how all his suffering, all his doing, all his life becomes delightful and happy, and it is a reward rather than a commandment. For the man who is so disposed has all he wants and wants nothing evil, and this is blessedness. Therefore our Lord says rightly: "Blessed are those who suffer for justice's sake."

Moreover, when our Lord, the Son, says: "Let him deny himself and take up his cross and follow me," this means: Become son as I am Son, born God, [become] the same One that I am, that I draw, indwelling and remaining, from the Father's bosom and heart. The Son says: "Father, I will that he who follows me and comes to me should be there where I am." No man comes in reality to the Son in as far as

39

he is Son, except him who becomes himself son, and no one is there where the Son is, who is in the Father's bosom and heart, one in one, except him who is son.

The Father says: "I will lead her into the desert and there speak to her heart." Heart to heart, one in one, that is what God loves. All that is foreign and far God hates; he entices and draws to the one. All creatures seek the one, even the lowest creatures seek the one, and the highest find the one; drawn and transformed above their nature, they seek the one in the one, the one in himself. Therefore probably the Son will say: In the Godhead, Son in the Father, where I am there shall be he who serves me, who follows me, who comes to me.

There is still another consolation. Saint Paul says that God chastises all those whom he takes and receives as sons. It belongs to being a son that one should also suffer. Because the Son of God could not suffer in his Godhead and in eternity, the heavenly Father sent him into time so that he should become man and be able to suffer. If, then, you would like to be God's son and yet not suffer, you are very wrong. It is written in the Book of Wisdom that God examines and searches who is just in the same way as gold is proved and burned in a furnace. It is a sign that the king or a prince trusts a knight well if he sends him into the combat. I have seen a lord who sometimes, when he had accepted someone among his followers, sent him out into the night and then attacked him himself and fought with him. And once it happened that he was nearly killed by someone whom he meant to try in this way, and he liked this man much better than before.

We read that Saint Anthony in the desert had once to suffer particularly bad temptations from the evil spirits, and when he had conquered his suffering, our Lord appeared to him visibly and joyfully. Then said the saintly man: "Ah, dear Lord, where were you just now, when I was in such great distress?" Then said our Lord: "I was here just as I am now. But I greatly desired to see how good you were." Silver and gold are indeed pure; yet, if they are to be made into a cup from which the king should drink, they would be burned very much more than otherwise. Therefore it is written of the apostles that they rejoiced to be found worthy to suffer ignominy for God.

He who was Son of God by nature willed to be man by grace, so that he might suffer for your sake, and you want to become the son of God and not man, in order that you may not and need not suffer either for God's sake or for your own?

If a man knew and considered how great joy God has himself according to his mode and all angels and all who know and love God, when they see the patience of a man who suffers sorrow and tribulation for God's sake, this alone should rightly console him. For surely a man gives his possessions and endures suffering so that he may give joy to his friend and do him a kindness.

We should further consider, if a man had a friend who was suffering pain and distress for his sake, it would surely be right that he should console him with his presence and with all the comfort he could give him. Therefore our Lord says in the Psalms of a good man that he is with him in his suffering.

From Sermons

This Is Meister Eckhart, from Whom God Hid Nothing
～ ～

For while all things were in quiet silence and the night was in the midst of her course. . . .
— WISDOM OF SOLOMON 18:14–15

Here in time we make holiday because the eternal birth which God the Father bore and bears unceasingly in eternity is now born in time, in human nature. Saint Augustine says this birth is always happening. But if it does not happen in me, what does it profit me? What matters is that it shall happen in me.

We intend therefore to speak of this birth as taking place in us, as being consummated in the virtuous soul, for it is in the perfect soul that God speaks his Word. What I shall say is true only of the perfected man, of him who has walked and is still walking in the way of God, not of the natural undisciplined man who is entirely remote from and unconscious of this birth.

There is a saying of the wise man, "When all

45

things lay in the midst of silence, then leapt there down into me from on high, from the royal throne, a secret word." This sermon is about this word.

Concerning it three things are to be noted. The first is, where in the soul God the Father speaks his Word, where she is receptive of this act, where this birth occurs. It is bound to be in the purest, loftiest, subtlest part of the soul. Truly if God the Father in his omnipotence had endowed the soul with a still nobler nature, had she received from him anything yet more exalted, then the Father would have delayed this birth for the presence of this greater excellence. The soul in which this birth happens must be absolutely pure and must live in gentle fashion, quite peaceful and wholly introverted; not running out through the five senses into the manifoldness of creatures, but altogether within and harmonized in her summit. That is its place. Anything inferior is disdained by it.

The second part of this discourse has to do with man's conduct in relation to this act, this interior speaking, this birth: whether it is more profitable to cooperate in it—perhaps by creating in the mind an imaginary image and disciplining oneself with it by reflecting that God is wise, omnipotent, eternal, or whatever else one is able to imagine about God—so that the birth may come to pass in us through our own exertion and merit, or whether it is more profitable and conducive to this birth from the Father to shun all thoughts, words, and deeds as well as all mental images and empty oneself, maintaining a wholly God-receptive attitude, such that one's own self is idle letting God work. Which conduct serves this birth best?

The third point is the profit, and how great it is, that accrues from this birth.

Note in the first place that in what I am about to say I intend to avail myself of natural proofs that you yourselves can grasp, for though I put more faith in the scriptures than myself, nevertheless it is easier and better for you to learn by means of arguments that can be verified.

First we will take the words, "In the midst of the silence there was spoken in me a secret word." But, sir, where is the silence and where the place in which the word is spoken?

As I said just now, it is in the purest part of the soul, in the noblest, in her ground, yes, in the very essence of the soul. That is mid-silence, for no creature ever entered there, nor any image, nor has the soul there either activity or understanding, therefore she is not aware of any image either of herself or any creature. Whatever the soul effects, she effects with her powers. When she understands, she understands with her intellect. When she remembers, she does so with her memory. When she loves, she does so with her will. She works then with her powers and not with her essence. Now every exterior act is linked with some means. The power of seeing is brought into play only through the eyes; elsewhere she can neither do nor bestow such a thing as seeing. And so with all the other senses: their operations are always effected through some means or other. But there is no activity in the essence of the soul; the faculties she works with emanate from the ground of the essence, but in her actual ground there is mid-stillness; here alone is rest and a habitation for this birth, this act, wherein God the Father speaks his Word, for it is intrinsically receptive of nothing but the divine essence, without means. Here God enters the soul with his all, not merely with a part. God enters the ground of the soul. None can touch the ground of the soul but God. No creature is admitted into her ground, it must stop outside in her powers. There it sees the image whereby it has been drawn in and found shelter. For when the soul's powers contact a creature, they set out to make of the creature an image and likeness which they absorb. By it they know the creature. Creatures cannot enter the soul, nor can the soul know anything about a creature whose image she has not willingly taken into herself. She approaches creatures through their present images, an image being a thing that the soul creates with her powers. Be it a stone, a rose, a man, or anything else that she wants to know about, she gets out the image of it which she has already taken in and is thus enabled to unite herself with it. But an image received in this way must of necessity enter from without through the senses. Consequently, there is nothing so unknown to the soul as herself. The soul, says a philosopher, can neither create nor absorb an image of herself. So she has nothing to know herself by. Images all enter through the senses, hence she can have no image of herself. She knows other things but not herself. Of nothing does she know so little as of herself, owing to this arrangement. Now you must know that inwardly the soul is free from means and images; that is why God can freely unite with her without form or image. You cannot but attribute to God without measure whatever power you attribute to a master. The wiser and more powerful the master, the more immediately is his work effected and the simpler it is. Man requires many instruments for his external works; much preparation is needed before he can bring them forth as he has imagined them. The sun and moon, whose work is to give light, in their mastership perform this very swiftly: the instant their radiance is poured forth, all the ends of the world are full of light. More exalted are the angels, who need less means for their works and have fewer images. The highest Seraph has but a single image. He seizes as a unity all that his inferiors regard as manifold. Now God needs no image and has no image: without image, likeness, or means does God work in the soul, in her ground wherein no image ever entered other than himself with his own essence. This no creature can do.

How does God the Father give birth to his Son in the soul—like creatures, in image and likeness? No, by my faith! But just as he gives him birth in eternity and not otherwise.

Well, but how does he give him birth there?

See. God the Father has perfect insight into himself, profound and thorough knowledge of himself by means of himself, not by means of any image. And thus God the Father gives birth to his Son in the very oneness of the divine nature. Thus it is and in no other way that God the Father gives birth to his Son in the ground and essence of the soul and thus he unites himself with her. Were any image present, there would not be real union, and in real union lies true bliss.

Now you may say: "But there is nothing innate in the soul but images." No, not so! If that were true, the soul would never be happy, for God cannot make any creature in which you could enjoy perfect happiness, otherwise God would not be the highest happiness and final goal, whereas it is his will and nature to be the alpha and omega of all. No creature can be happiness. And here indeed can just as little be perfection, for perfection (perfect virtue, that is to say) results from perfection of life. Therefore you truly must sojourn and dwell in your essence, in your ground, and there God shall mix you with his simple essence without the medium of any image. No image represents and signifies itself: it stands for that of which it is the image. Now seeing that you have no image other than what is outside you, therefore it is impossible for you to be beatified by any image whatsoever.

The second point is, what does it behoove a man to do in order to deserve and procure this birth to come to pass and be consummated in him? Is it better for him to do his part toward it, to imagine and think about God, or should he keep still in peace and quiet so that God can speak and act in him while he merely waits on God's operation? At the same time I repeat that this speaking, this act, is only for the good and perfect, those who have so absorbed and assimilated the essence of virtue that it emanates from them naturally, without their seeking; and above all there must live in them the worthy life and lofty teaching of our Lord Jesus Christ. Such are permitted to know that the very best and utmost of attainment in this life is to remain still and let God act and speak in you. When the powers have all been withdrawn from their bodily forms and functions, then this Word is spoken. Thus he says: "in the midst of the silence the secret word was spoken to me." The more completely you are able to draw in your faculties and forget those things and their images which you have taken in, the more, that is to say, you forget the creature, the nearer you are to this and the more susceptible you are to it. If only you could suddenly be altogether unaware of things, could you but pass into oblivion of your own existence as Saint Paul did when he said: "Whether in the body I know not, or out of the body I know not, God knows!" Here the spirit had so entirely absorbed the faculties that it had forgotten the body: memory no longer functioned, nor understanding, nor the senses, nor even those powers whose duty it is to govern and grace the body; vital warmth and energy were arrested so that the body remained intact throughout the three days during which he neither ate nor drank. It was the same with Moses when he fasted forty days on the mount and was none the worse for it: on the last day he was as strong as on the first. Thus a man must abscond from his senses, invert his faculties, and lapse into oblivion of things and of himself. About which a philosopher addressed the soul: "Withdraw from the restlessness of external activities!" And again: "Flee away and hide from the turmoil of outward occupations and inward thoughts, for they create nothing but discord!" If God is to speak his Word in the soul, she must be at rest and at peace; then he speaks in the soul his Word and himself: not an image but himself. Dionysius says: "God has no image nor likeness of himself, seeing that he is intrinsically all good, truth, and being." God performs all his works in himself and outside himself simultaneously. Do not fondly imagine that God, when he created the heavens and the earth and all creatures, made one thing one day and another the next. Moses describes it thus, nevertheless he knew better: he did so merely on account of those who are incapable of understanding or conceiving otherwise. All God did was: he willed and they were. God works without instrument and without image. And the freer you are from images, the more receptive you are to his interior operation, and the more introverted and oblivious you are, the closer you are to it. Dionysius exhorted his disciple Timothy in this sense, saying, "Dear son Timothy, with untroubled mind swing yourself up above yourself and above your powers, above all modes and all existences, into the secret, still darkness, that you may attain to the knowledge of the unknown super-divine God." All things must be forsaken. God scorns to work among images.

Now you may say, "What is it that God does without images in the ground and essence?" That I am incapable of knowing, for my soul powers can receive only in images; they have to recognize and lay hold of each thing in its appropriate image: they cannot recognize a bird in the image of a man. Now since images all enter from without, this is concealed from my soul, which is most salutary for her. Not knowing makes her wonder and leads her to eager pursuit, for she knows clearly *that* it is but knows not *how* nor *what* it is. No sooner does a man know the reason of a thing than immediately he tires of it and goes casting about for something new. Always clamoring to know, he is ever inconstant. The soul is constant only to this unknowing knowing which keeps her pursuing.

The wise man said concerning this: "In the middle of the night when all things were in quiet silence, there was spoken to me a hidden word." It came like a thief, by stealth. What does he mean by a word that was hidden? The nature of a word is to reveal what is hidden. It appeared before me, shining out with intent to reveal and giving me knowledge of God. Hence it is called a word. But what it was remained hidden from me. That was its stealthy coming "in a whispering stillness to reveal itself." It is just because it is hidden that one is and must be always after it. It appears and disappears; we are meant to yearn and sigh for it.

Saint Paul says we ought to pursue this until we spy it and not stop until we grasp it. When he returned after having been caught up into the third heaven where God was made known to him and where he beheld all things, he had forgotten nothing, but it was so deep down in his ground that his intellect could not reach it; it was veiled from him. He was therefore obliged to pursue it and search for it in himself, not outside himself. It is not outside, it is inside: wholly within. And being convinced of this, he said, "I am sure that neither death nor any affliction can separate me from what I find within me."

There is a fine saying of one heathen philosopher to another about this. He says; "I am aware of something in me which sparkles in my intelligence; I clearly perceive *that* it is something, but *what* I cannot grasp. Yet it seems if I could only seize it I should know all truth." To which the other philosopher replied, "Follow it boldly! For if you can seize it, you will possess the sum total of all good and have eternal life!" Saint Augustine expresses himself in the same sense: "I am conscious of something within me that plays before my soul and is as a light dancing in front of it; were this brought to steadiness and perfection in me, it would surely be eternal life!" It hides yet it shows. It comes, but after the manner of a thief, with intent to take and to steal all things from the soul. By emerging and showing itself somewhat, it purposes to decoy the soul and draw it toward itself to rob it and take itself from it. As the prophet said: "Lord take from them their spirit and give them instead thy spirit." This too the loving soul meant when she said, "My soul dissolved and melted away when Love spoke his word; when he entered I could not but fail." And Christ signified it by his words: "Whosoever shall leave anything for my sake shall be repaid a hundredfold, and whosoever will possess me must deny himself and all things, and whosoever will serve me must follow me nor go anymore after his own."

Now perhaps you will say, "But, sir, you are

wanting to change the natural course of the soul! It is her nature to take in through the senses, in images. Would you upset this arrangement?" No! But how do you know what nobility God has bestowed on human nature, what perfections yet uncatalogued, even undiscovered? Those who have written of the soul's nobility have gone no further than their natural intelligence could carry them: they never entered her ground, so that much remained obscure and unknown to them. "I will sit in silence and hearken to what God speaks within me," said the prophet. Into this retirement steals the Word in the darkness of the night. Saint John says, "The light shines in the darkness; it came unto its own and as many as received it became in authority sons of God: to them was given power to become God's sons."

Notice the fruit and use of this mysterious Word and of this darkness. In this gloom which is his own, the heavenly Father's Son is not born alone: you too are born there a child of the same heavenly Father and no other, and to you also he gives power. Observe how great the use. No truth learned by any master by his own intellect and understanding, or ever to be learned this side of the day of judgment, has ever been interpreted at all according to this knowledge, in this ground. Call it if you will an ignorance, an unknowing, yet there is in it more than in all knowing and understanding without it, for this outward ignorance lures and attracts you from all understood things and from yourself. This is what Christ meant when he said, "Whosoever denies not himself and leaves not father and mother and is not estranged from all these, he is not worthy of me." As though to say: he who abandons not creaturely externals can neither be conceived nor born in this divine birth. But divesting yourself of yourself and of everything external does indeed give it to you. And in very truth I believe, no, I am sure, that the man who is established here can in no way be at any time separated from God. I hold he can in no way lapse into mortal sin. He would rather suffer the most shameful death, as the saints have done before him, than commit the least of mortal sins. I hold that he cannot willingly commit, nor yet consent to, even a venial sin, whether in himself or in another. So strongly is he drawn and attracted to this way, so much is he habituated to it, that he could never turn to any other; to this way are directed all his senses, all his powers.

May the God who has been born again as man assist us in this birth, continually helping us, weak men, to be born again in him as God. Amen.

Innocents' Day

Dear children you must know that true spiritual life leads to perfect freedom from self and from all things. One cares nothing, seeks nothing, has nothing, wants nothing for oneself, but frankly resigns oneself to the eternal law, always so clearly shown to the discerning but which none may know unless he is inwardly atoned and outwardly obedient to the discipline perfectly exemplified in our Lord Jesus Christ. Those who live this life, they verily attain to unity, and to know the truth one has to dwell in unity and be the unity. He who is at all aware of his own mind knows and conceives nothing of God's. By the fact of his knowing and seeing, he is not void. The highest knowing and seeing is knowing and seeing, unknowing, unseeing. To know anything of self is to know nothing of God, and he who wants God to be his is putting an obstacle in his own way. "He who wants God to be his is in danger of spiritual pride," so says one of the saints. With the righteous soul, the more God is to her the less he is hers, for God is all his own. The right humble spirit is little in itself, because the way of truth is made known to it. True spiritual poverty leads into it. The soul will find no more profound humility than that of our Lord Jesus Christ, who himself declared, "I am not of myself."

On Luke 14:16

A man once gave a great banquet and invited many; . . .

—LUKE 14:16

If one gives a dinner in the morning, one invites all sorts of people, but for an evening meal one invites distinguished guests, those dear to one, and intimate friends.

Today Christendom celebrates the day of the Last Supper, which our Lord gave for his disciples, his familiar friends, when he gave them his sacred Body for their food. This is the first meaning. A further meaning of the Last Supper is this: before evening comes, there must be a morning and a noon. The divine Light rises in the soul and produces a morning, and in this Light the soul mounts up into a breadth and a height, into noon: then follows evening. Now we would speak again in a different sense about evening. Evening comes when the light disappears; when the whole world falls away from the soul, then it is evening, then the soul finds rest. Now Saint Gregory says about the Last Supper: If one eats in the

61

morning there follows another meal; but after supper there is no other meal. When, at the [Eucharistic] Supper, the soul tastes the food and the spark of the soul seizes on the divine Light, then it needs no other food and seeks nothing outside and stays altogether in the divine Light. Now Saint Augustine says: Lord, if you take yourself away from us, give us another you; we find no satisfaction in anything except you, for we want nothing but you. Our Lord took himself away from his disciples as God and Man, and he gave himself back to them as God and Man, but in another mode and in another form. As it is done where there is a very sacred object: one does not let it be seen or touched without a cover; it is encased in crystal or something else. Thus did also our Lord, when he gave himself as another himself. In the Last Supper God gives himself with all he is as food for his dear friends. Saint Augustine was terrified of this food; then a voice said to him in his mind, "I am food for adults; grow and increase and eat me! You will not change me into yourself, but you will be changed into me." Of the food and drink I took a fortnight ago, a power of my soul took the purest and subtlest element, introduced it into my body, and united it with all that is in it, so that there is nothing even as small as what would fit on a needle that has not been united with me; and it is so actually one with me as that which was conceived in my mother's womb when life was first infused into me. Just as really the power of the Holy Spirit takes what is purest and most subtle and sublime, the spark of the soul, and carries it all upward in the burning fire, in love, as I now say of the tree: the power of the sun takes what is purest and most subtle in the root of the tree and draws it right up into the branch where it becomes a blossom. In exactly the same way the spark in the soul is borne up in the light and the Holy Spirit, and is thus carried into the first origin and becomes wholly one with God and so tends wholly into the One and is in a more real sense one with God than is the food with my body, indeed very much more, in that it is much purer and nobler. Therefore he says, "A great banquet." Now David says, "Lord, how great and varied is the sweetness and the food which you have hidden for all those who fear you"; and if a man receives this food with fear, it will never really taste good to him; it must be received with love. Hence a soul that loves God conquers God so that he must altogether give himself to it.

Now Saint Luke says, "A man made a great banquet." This man had no name, this man had no equal, this man is God. God has no name. A pagan master says that no tongue can say an adequate word of God, because of the sublimity and purity of his being. If we speak of a tree, we make statements about it through the things that are above the tree, such as the sun that acts on the tree. Therefore we cannot speak of God in a true sense, because there is nothing above God, and God has no cause. Secondly, we make statements about things by means of similarity. Therefore one cannot really speak of God because nothing is equal to him. Thirdly, we make statements about things according to their operations: if one wants to speak about the art of a master, one speaks of the image he has created: the image reveals the master's art. All the creatures are too inferior to reveal God, all of them are nought compared with God. This is why no creature is capable of uttering one single word about God through the things he has created. Hence Dionysius says: All those who want to make statements about God are wrong, for they fail to say anything about him. Those who want to say nothing about him are right, for no word can express God; but he expresses himself in himself. Therefore David says, "In thy light shall we see light." Luke says, "A man." He is one and he is a man, and he is equal to none and transcends all.

The Love of God

In this was manifested the love of God toward us, because that God sent his only begotten Son into the world, that we might live [with him, in him, and] through him.

— I JOHN 4:9

Suppose that a rich king had a beautiful daughter and gave her to the son of a poor man. Every member of the poor family would be honored and ennobled by the gift. There is one authority who says: "Since God became man, the whole human race has been lifted up and ennobled—wherefore we may all rejoice that Christ, our brother, of his own power, has risen above the choir of angels to sit at the right hand of God the Father." This is well said, but even then, it does not mean much to me. For what good would it do me to have a brother who is rich, while I remain poor, or a brother wise, when I am foolish? I should rather put it this way, and say, not only that God became man, but that he has taken human nature upon himself—for this is more to the point.

Authorities usually teach that all persons are of

65

equal rank by nature, but I say emphatically that all the worth of the humanity of the saints, or Mary, the mother of God, or even Christ himself, is mine too in my human nature. But this might prompt you to ask: If, in my present nature, I already have all that Christ achieved in his, why should he be exalted and honored as the Lord and God? Because he was a messenger from God to us, who carried a blessing that was to be ours. There in the inmost core of the soul, where God begets his Son, human nature also takes root. There, too, it is one and unanalyzable. Anything that might appear to belong to it, and yet could be distinguished from it, would not be of that unity. But now I shall say something further that is more difficult. To live by this pure essence of our nature, one must be so dead to all that is personal that he could be as fond of persons long dead as he is of familiar and homely friends. As long as you are more concerned for yourself than you are for people you have never seen, you are wrong, and you cannot have even a momentary insight into the simple core of the soul. You may have a symbolic idea of the truth, but this is by no means best.

In the second place, you must be pure in heart, for his heart alone is pure for whom creatures are as nothing.

In the third place, you must have got rid of all "Not."

They ask, what is burned in hell? Authorities usually reply: "This is what happens to willfulness." But I say it is this "Not" that is burned out in hell. For example: suppose a burning coal is placed on my hand. If I say that the coal burns me, I do it a great injustice. To say precisely what does the burning: it is the "Not." The coal has something in it that my hand has not. Observe! It is just this "Not" that is burning me—for if my hand had in it what the coal has, and could do what the coal can do, it too would blaze with fire, in which case all the fire that ever burned might be spilled on this hand and I should not feel hurt.

Likewise, I should say that because God and all who live in his presence have something like true blessedness in them, such as those who are cut off from God have not, it is only the "Not" [the need or want of blessing] that punishes souls in hell, rather than any willfulness or other kind of fuel. Truly I say that to the extent "Not" exists in you, you are imperfect, and if you would be perfect you must get rid of it.

Thus my text says: "God sent his only begotten Son into the world"—and by that you must not understand the external world, in which he ate and drank with us, but you should know that it refers to the inner world. As sure as the Father, so single in nature, begets his Son, he begets him in the spirit's inmost recess—and that is the inner world. Here, the core of God is also my core; and the core of my soul, the core of God's, and here, I am independent as God himself is independent. If one could peek into this core [of the soul] even for an instant, he would afterward think no more of a thousand pounds of beaten red gold than of a counterfeit farthing.

Do all you do, acting from the core of your soul, without a single "Why." I tell you, whenever what you do is done for the sake of the Kingdom of God, or for God's sake, or for eternal blessing, and thus really for ulterior motives, you are wrong. You may pass for a good person, but this is not the best. For, truly, if you imagine that you are going to get more out of God by means of religious offices and devotions, in sweet retreats and solitary orisons, than you might by the fireplace or in the stable, then you might just as well think you could seize God and wrap a mantle around his head and stick him under the table! To seek God by rituals is to get the ritual and lose God in the process, for he hides behind it. On the other hand, to seek God without artifice is to take him as he is, and so doing, a person "lives by the Son," and is the Life itself.

For if Life were questioned a thousand years and asked: "Why live?" and if there were an answer, it could be no more than this: "I live only to live!" And that is because Life is its own reason for being, springs from its own Source, and goes on and on, without ever asking why—just because it is life. Thus, if you ask a genuine person, that is, one who acts [uncalculatingly] from his heart: "Why are you doing that?"—he will reply in the only possible way: "I do it because I do it!"

Where the creature ends, there God begins to be. God asks only that you get out of his way, insofar as you are creature, and let him be God in you. The least creaturely idea that ever entered your mind is as big as God. Why? Because it will keep God out of you entirely. The moment you get [one of your own] ideas, God fades out and the Godhead too. It is when the idea is gone that God gets in.

God desires urgently that you, the creature, get out of his way—as if his own blessedness depended on it. Ah, beloved people, why don't you let God be God in you? What are you afraid of? You get completely out of his way and he will get out of yours— you give up to him and he will give up to you. When both [God and you] have forsaken self, what remains [between you] is an indivisible union. It is in this unity that the Father begets his Son in the secret spring of your nature. Then the Holy Spirit blooms and out of God there comes a will which belongs to the soul. As long as this will remains uncorrupted by creatures, it is free. Christ says: "No man rises to heaven but he that came from heaven." All things were created out of nothingness and thus their true origin is the "Not." That is why the aristocratic [free] will, to the extent it condescends to created things, lapses at last with them to their nothingness.

It is sometimes asked whether this noble will may lapse so completely that it cannot recover. The authorities usually teach that, if it has lapsed for some time, there is no recovery. But I say, if [your] will is directed back again, to its secret source, it will once again be as it was, formally free and really free, and at once all the time that was lost will be made up.

People often say to me: "Pray for me!" At that I have to wonder: Why did you ever leave him? And why not be your true self and reach into your own treasure? For the whole truth is just as much in you as in me!

That we all may similarly remain close to this treasure, that we all may know the truth blessedly, without anything separating us from it, or standing in between, may God help! Amen.

Poverty

The really virtuous man does not need God. What I have I don't lack. He makes no plans, he sets no store by things. As God is higher than man, so is he readier to give than man is to receive. Not by his fasts and vigils and his many outward works does a man prove his progress in the virtuous life, but it is a sure sign of his growth if he finds eternal things more and more attractive than the things that pass. The man who has a thousand marks of gold and gives it all away for love of God is doing a fine thing, yet I say, it were far finer and far better for him to despise it, regarding it as nothing on God's account.

A man should orient his will and all his works to God and having only God in view go forward unafraid, not thinking, am I right or am I wrong? One who worked out all the chances before starting his first fight would never fight at all. And if, going to some place, we must think how to set the front foot down, we shall never get there. It is our duty to do the next thing: go straight on, that is the right way.

There are five kinds of poverty: the first is devilish poverty; the second, golden poverty; the third is willing poverty; the fourth is spiritual poverty; the fifth, divine poverty.

The first, or devilish poverty, applies to all who have not what they wish to have, outwardly or inwardly. That is their hell.

The second, golden poverty, is theirs who in the midst of goods and properties pass empty without and within. If everything they own were burnt, the effect on them would be to leave them quite unmoved. Heaven would be theirs and they would have no less.

The third is willing poverty and belongs to those who, renouncing goods and honors, body and soul, leave everything with right good grace. These give judgment with the twelve apostles and by pronouncing judgment it is their judgment day who, knowing what they leave, yet set another in their heart and mightily stir themselves up about their own departure. Such are the willing poor.

The fourth are spiritually poor. These have forsaken friends and kindred, not merely goods and honor, body and soul; further, they have given up all good works; the eternal Word does all their work while they are idle and exempt from all activity. And since in the eternal Word is neither bad nor good, therefore they are absolutely empty.

The fifth are godly poor, for God can find no place in them to work. Theirs is riddance without and within, for they are bare and free from all contingent form. This is the man: in this man all men are one man, and that man is Christ. Of him one master says, "Earth was never worthy of this man who looks on heaven and earth the same." This man is object-free in time and in eternity.

Now enough of those who have no object in eternity, but one thing more of those who are objectless in time. What is meant by object? There are two objects: one is otherness (not I); the other is a man's own proper self (his I).

The first otherness is *becoming,* all that has come into existence; such things breed otherness and pass away. This applies to the passage of time.

He who knows one matter in all things remains unmoved. For matter is the subject of form, and there can be no matter without form nor form devoid of matter. Form without matter is nothing at all, but matter ever cleaves to form and is one undivided whole in every single part of it. Now since form in itself is nothing, therefore it moves nothing. And since matter is perfectly indivisible, therefore it is unmoved. This man then is unmoved by form or matter and is therefore objectless in time.

Man's other object is to possess his proper self, to identify himself with all perfection, with that most precious treasure of his own: that is his quest. Now when a thing has gotten its own form, no more nor less, that thing is all its own and no one else's. He who conceives this really is perfect in the sense that he is wholly objectless to eternity.

What Mary Was Doing When the Angel Came

⤔ ⤕

He of Sterngassen said, I am often asked what Our Lady was doing when the angel came to her. Twenty-one things are predicated of her. She was sitting in time untimely. She was sitting, a creature uncreaturely. She was sitting in the body maidenly. Her soul was deiform. Her spirit was contemplating God. Her mind was heavenly calm. Her outward life was altogether lovely. Her soul was generous. To her nothing at all under God was of any account. Her heart was aflame with the truth. Clear consciousness was her school. Heaven was her cell. Divinity was her reading. Eternal truth was her mentor. She had no inclination toward creatures but was simply bent upon God. She was liberated from creatures and set upon God alone. Her spirit was inspired with the Spirit of God. In body on the earth her spirit was in heaven. She was in the land of freedom. Where lies the land of freedom? In complete detachment from creatures, and in the land of freedom lies the state of purity. She sat in the cell of recollection and dispassion. She sat in the house of godly certitude. She sat in the school of the Trinity and heard what the schoolmaster of truth was saying. In the darkness she saw a light. In the silence she heard a word. In passivity she was aware of activity. Her soul was all the time resting in eternity and abiding in the Godhead, and she was satisfied with the divine perfection.

Peace

Jesus came and stood among them and said to them, "Peace be with you."

—JOHN 20:19

Saint John tells us in his gospel that "on the first day of the week, at evening, when the doors were shut, came our Lord and stood in the midst of the disciples and said, "Peace be with you!" and again, "Peace be with you!" and a third time, "Receive the Holy Ghost!" Now the evening never comes unless morning and midday have gone before. We say that the middle of the day is warmer than the evening. But insofar as evening takes in midday and stores up its heat, it is the warmer; when, too, before the evening there goes a whole bright day. Late in the year, again, after the summer solstice, when the sun is drawing near to earth, the evenings will grow warm. But midday never comes till morning goes, nor evening until noon has passed away. The moral of which is, that when the divine light breaks forth in the soul, getting brighter and brighter unto the perfect day, then morning does not vanish before noon nor noon before evening: they close up to one. So the evening is warm. There is perfect day in the soul when all the soul is full of light divine. But it is evening in the soul, as I have said before, when the light of this world fades and the soul goes in to rest.

God said, "Peace!" and "Peace!" again, and "Receive the Holy Ghost!" Jacob the patriarch came to a place in the evening and, putting underneath his head some stones which lay about, he sank to rest. In his sleep he saw a ladder reaching up to heaven with angels ascending and descending and God leaning down over the top of the ladder. This place Jacob slept in had no name. Which is as much as to say the Godhead alone is the place of the soul, and is nameless. Concerning this our doctors say: a thing which is another's place must be above it, as heaven is the place of all things and fire is the place of air and air the place of water and water, partially, the place of earth, and earth is not a place. An angel is a heavenly place, and any angel who has got the least drop more of God than any other is the place, the habitation, of that other, the most exalted angel being the place, the room, the measure of the rest while he himself is without measure. But although he is without measure, nonetheless God is his measure.

Jacob rested in the place which is nameless. By

not naming it, it is named. On getting to this name-less place the soul will rest, where all things are being God in God, there shall she rest. The abode of the soul, which God is, is unnamed. I say, God is unspo-ken. But Saint Augustine says that God is not unspo-ken; were he unspoken, even that would be speech, and he is more silence than speech. One of our most ancient philosophers who found the truth long, long before God's birth, before there ever was Christian faith at all as it is now, to him (I say) it seemed that what he could manage to utter of things only con-jured up within him something monstrous and un-real, and therefore he refused to speak at all. Not even would he say, give me meat or give me drink. He declined to mention things because he could not say them as perfect as they sprang from their first cause; he chose rather to be dumb and to make known his wants by pointing with his finger. How much more does it suit us, if he knew not the way to talk of things, to be absolutely mute concerning him who is the origin of all things.

We say that God is a spirit. Not so. If God were really a spirit, he would be spoken. According to Saint Gregory, we cannot rightly speak of God at all. Anything we say of him is bound to be a stammering. This place which is not named, wherein all creatures thrive and bloom in orderly array, this habitat of all creatures, is gotten suddenly out of the ground of this orderly place, the seat of the soul proceeding out of this ground.

TEMPLVM·DOMINI

The Spark

~ ~

O sweet nature of the unborn light, purify my mind
and enlighten my understanding so that I may be conscious of you!

Christ said, My Father has sent me to preach the
gospel to the poor. Bishop Albertus says God is in all
things (that is, in the soul). He has endowed her with
virtues and with the wisdom which is in God, so that
this wisdom is confined to himself. Saint John says we
know that we love because we love without means.
The Father is to us in his heart as he has been to us in
his Son. Saint Augustine cries, Lord I cannot love
you, but come in and love yourself in me. According
to Saint Paul, we must put off our own natural form
and put on the form of God, and Saint Augustine tells
us to discard our own mode of nature; then the divine
nature will flow in and be revealed. Saint Augustine
says, Those who seek and find, find not. He who
seeks and finds not, he alone finds. Saint Paul says,
What I was, was not I, it was God in me. And Saint
Paul declares that we are messengers or servants of
the Spirit. Saint Augustine cries, I who have always
been in God and ever more shall be, would sooner I
had never been and nevermore should be than that we

could understand a single word my Father God might say. Saint Bernard tells us to follow where God leads. Soaring wishes lose us what we have and fail to bring us what we want.

Saint John the Baptist was asked by his disciples, Where shall we go to see him? He answered, Why should I go and see in the flesh what I see spiritually? Saint John most pregnantly affirms, The light is from the light and God from God. The Son is born of the substance of the Father. Wisdom says in her book, before the heavens and earth were made, I emerged from the Supreme in eternal birth. Further, Wisdom says, I have caused to be born for you in the heavens a light that shall never go out.

Philosophers declare concerning the inner senses that these are of two kinds, the highest and the lowest. The lowest come between the highest and the outward senses, and to these outer ones are near allied. What the eye sees or the ear hears is straightaway seized by desire, provided it pleases, and conveyed to the critical faculty which considers it well and, if lawful, passes it on to the superior powers, which take it and carry it up to the chief power, without likeness, for this power admits neither image nor likeness. It is called *sinderesis,* and is all one with the soul's nature, a spark of the divine nature. It cannot abide what is not good. It is without stain; perfectly pure and wholly superior to temporal things, it dwells in unchanging stability, like eternity. Anything that enters here must first be freed from multiplicity and sensible affections. The powers of the soul, outer and inner, are all summed up in this, and whatever gets into this highest power it passes on to all the rest, an act eternal in its nature; it is so quick, it is practically timeless.

A heathen master says, That heart is pure which will not countenance a thing just because the world likes it. According to one of the saints, creatures which God has given us for a stepladder to God we have ourselves made into an offense by stopping in them on our way to safety. A heathen philospher says the *mens* is very pure, and if it loses nothing here, neither does it elsewhere. Comparing like with like, there is not much to choose, very little indeed, except that you bring in more awareness than you had in your First Cause. A subtler heathen suggests that what we know of the First Cause is rather what we are ourselves than what the First Cause is, for that passes all understanding.

According to Gregory and Origen, that man denies himself who from stubbornness changes to perfect humility, from greed to despisery of earthly things, and who, resigning his own will, endeavors to promote the will of God rather than his own felicity, and this with no hope of reward. In order to abide in a constant state of unity, all this has to go. Work must be done simply for the work's sake and not for any why. One heathen philosopher claims that whatever you work at, whatever you do, if it wrests you from pride and multiplicity to humility and unity, without doubt it is good. Boëthius counsels, If you would know the naked truth, then cast off joy and fear and faith and hope and pain and qualities in general; all of them are means. As a heathen philosopher says, Discard all this and that and here and now and be yourself as you are in your innermost nature.

Outcast from his Father's home is he who governs not himself and follows not the true inner light. Amen.

The Beatific Vision

"Behold I make all things new." Saint John says this in the Book of Revelation, and we read it at the annual church festival. Augustine says it is good to seek the will of God, and asks, "Why does God do so and so?" But to seek the cause of the will of God is to seek something prior to, higher than God, whose will is himself. He who seeks nothing shall find nothing. Beware then of human curiosity, lest seeking what is nothing, we lose the something which is eternal. Although now we see no cause why God created creatures, yet we have some indication in the fact that creatures, various angels, and some men have exuberant delight in the three Persons, in their eternal intercourse and uses, in the intellectual vision of God's essential nature, in the undefined real presence of the formless form of divine Being. In the highest light of mental gnosis, therein the ground of beatitude lies. Accordingly there springs up and grows within the will a prelude of delights which the vision adorns as bloom does youth, and therein is revealed to all creatures the splendor and majesty of his estate, and concerning it he says, "Behold I make all things new." Our annual festival commemorates the eternal happening depicted here. But since God has specially designed his joys for the human soul, that she may be happy in him, therefore the words apply to us in two particulars. First, to the noble nature of the soul, for he calls the soul by the name of all things. The second reference is to the natural end of the soul (perfection), which consists in bringing the soul, by knowing and loving, face to face with unveiled divine nature. And this he does for us in the renewing of the soul.

Now mark in the first place how the soul is all things. She has being with the stones and growing with the trees and feeling with the beasts and understanding with the angels. Moreover, she is just the same apart from form and intellect. According to the author of the book *On the First Cause,* the soul is created on the confines of eternity and time, so she sees into both and contains them both intelligibly. All things lead up to man. God made man last of all his creatures, on the sixth day, and was pleased thereon to feast his eyes, for in the soul he recognized his own reflection. Again, we might doctrinally liken the soul to all things, for the soul can win the blessings and rewards of all deserving creatures, as we see especially with the soul of Christ and of our Lady, more even than the angels. For the soul goes on growing without end. Also, when the soul has deserved reward of the rewarding grace of Christ, the bestowal has been wholly disproportionate, so that no creature can of its own nature see true in the mirror of God's nature, not even angels of the highest choir, excepting one soul, Christ's. Wherefore our Lord says, "And I if I am lifted up from earth will draw all things to me," meaning the soul.

Then, as to the renewal of the soul. Here you must bear in mind that what is new is near to its beginning. The fount of the soul is the eternal outpouring from the Father's heart, in form that is. But causally all, the whole Trinity, is the source; not the Persons in their separate reflections but in their perfect community of essence with, besides, the purpose of the will of God as dictated by the eternal law of wisdom, otherwise the soul would be eternal like her source, which the faith denies. God says he will draw the soul to him, and she shall be made new, for she has wandered far from him and, in the death throes of unlikeness caused by the assaults of lethal things, has lost her pristine bloom, her first God–given freshness. Then the soul can say in spirit with the prophet, "My youth is renewed like the eagle's and my life is blossoming afresh in God." This is due to the precept and the practice of the seven virtues, the six works of mercy, the eight beatitudes, and the twelve fruits of the Holy Ghost. Up then, glad soul, renew yourself! You can do it in this world. Not that God's plan is this alone, for in this life there is not yet finished even the first festival of dedication; its pattern of perfection is in the exalted Godhead. There God renews the soul, restoring her to her original rank, and purifies her powers from all traces of mortality and sets her in the light of glory. Then God renews the soul so that the soul beholds herself in the pure being of God: herself, I say, as herself, blessed and really existent, natural and spiritual, that is to say. Thereafter she beholds herself not as herself: she sees herself in God as eternal and divine. Thirdly, God finally renews the soul when in ever-new fresh-springing glory he presents himself to the intellect, and to desire as longing fulfilled, so the soul is ever thirsting and at the same time drinking. Then the soul is drenched in divine nature, then she receives divine light.

The Nobleman

Our Lord says in the Gospel: "A certain nobleman went out into a far country to receive for himself a kingdom, and returned." In these words our Lord teaches us how noble man is by nature and how divine is that to which he may attain by grace. In these words too we have the theme of the major part of holy scripture.

To start with, you must know and it is manifest that man has in him two natures: body and spirit. Hence it has been said: He who knows himself will know all creatures, for creatures are all either body or spirit. Accordingly the scriptures say of human beings that there is in us one man outwardly and another man within. To the outward man belong the dependents of the soul which are concerned and entangled with the flesh, which have a work in common with the organs of the body—the eye for instance, or the ear, the tongue, the hand, and so forth. The scriptures call all this the old man, the earthly man, the outward man, the enemy, the servant.

The other man, within us, is the inner man. The scriptures call him the new man, the heavenly man, the young man, the friend, the nobleman. It is of him that our Lord says, "A nobleman went out into a far country."

Further, you must know that Saint Gregory

says, and so with one accord do all the philosophers, that every man by the very fact of his being
a man has a good genius, an angel, and a bad genius, a devil. The good angel counsels and tends
without ceasing to good, to things godly, things
virtuous and heavenly and eternal. The bad genius
counsels and tends all the while to things temporal,
impermanent, vicious, devilish, and evil. This same
evil genius is forever parleying with the outward
man, and through him succeeds in covertly getting
at the inner man—just as the serpent became
friendly with the woman Eve and through her with
her husband, Adam. Adam is the inner man, the
man in the soul. He is the good tree of which our
Lord said that it always brought forth good fruit.
He is also the field wherein God has sowed his image and likeness and is sowing good seed, the root
of all wisdom, all knowledge, all virtue, all goodness, the seed of divine nature. This seed is God's
Son, God's Word.

The outward man is the enemy, the wicked man
who sows tares on the field. Of him Saint Paul says:
"I find within me hindrance and opposition to God's
command and counsel"—to what God has said and
keeps on saying in the ground and summit of my
soul. Elsewhere he cries, "O wretched man that I am!

Who shall deliver me from the body of my mortal flesh?" And in another place he speaks of man's spirit and his flesh always warring with each other. Flesh counseling vice and evil, spirit counseling love of God, peace, joy, and every virtue. He who is obedient and lives according to the spirit, to its teaching, to him belongs eternal life. He who is obedient to the flesh shall die. It is the inner man, the one of whom our Lord declares that he is the good tree, which always bears good fruit and never evil, for he wants goodness, is inclined to goodness, to goodness in itself all unconcerned with this and that. The outer man is the bad tree which can never bear good fruit.

As to the nobility of the inner spiritual man and the baseness of the carnal man, the heathen philosophers Tullius and Seneca maintain that there is no rational soul without God; the seed of God exists in us. Given a hard worker and a good director, it thrives apace and grows up into God whose seed it is, and its fruit is likewise God's nature. Pear seed grows up into pear tree, nut seed grows up into nut tree—God seed into God, to God. But if the good seed has a lazy worker and an incompetent director, then weeds spring up and strangle that good seed and by shutting out the light prevent it growing. And yet, says Origen, a great authority, "Since God himself has sown, dropped in, and gotten into us this seed, therefore it may be covered up and lost to view, but it can never be destroyed or die out in itself; it glows and sparkles, lightens and burns, always making for God.

In the first stage the inner or new man, Saint Augustine says, follows in the footsteps of good, pious people. He is still an infant at his mother's breast.

In the second stage he no longer follows blindly the example even of good people. He goes in hot pursuit of sound instruction, godly counsel, holy wisdom. He turns his back on man and his face to God; leaving his mother's lap he smiles to his heavenly Father.

In the third stage he parts more and more from his mother, draws further and further away from her breast. He flees care and casts away fear. Though he might with impunity treat everyone with harshness and injustice, he would find no satisfaction in it, for in his love to God he is so much engaged with him, so much occupied with him in doing good; God has established him so firmly in joy, in holiness and love that everything unlike and foreign to God seems to him unworthy and repugnant.

In the fourth stage he more and more grows and is rooted in love, in God. He is ever ready to welcome

any struggle, any trial, adversity, or suffering, and
that willingly, gladly, joyfully.

In the fifth stage he is at peace, enjoying the fullness of supreme ineffable wisdom.

In the sixth stage he is de-formed and transformed
by God's eternal nature. He has come to full perfection and, oblivious of impermanent things and temporal life, is drawn, transported, into the image of
God and become a child of God. There is no further
and no higher stage. It is eternal rest and bliss. The
end of the inner and new man is eternal life.

As to this inner noble man in whom God's form
is stamped, in whom God's seed is sown, how this
seed and exemplar of God's nature and God's essence,
God's Son, appears, and one grows aware of him, and
how he sometimes disappears—to this Origen, that
great authority, suggests a parallel: that God's Son,
God's image, is in the ground of the soul like a living
spring. If earth is thrown on it, earthly desire that is,
it smothers it, covers it over, and it vanishes from our
ken. But in itself it remains alive, and on removing
the soil that was thrown on from without, we see it
again. He notes how this truth is set forth in the First
Book of Moses, where we read that Abraham had
dug wells in his field and that evildoers had filled

them with earth, and when the earth was thrown out, the living stream reappeared.

To use another simile: the sun is always shining, but when there is a cloud or mist between us and the sun, we do not see its brightness, nor when the eyes are diseased or blind can they see its light. I sometimes use this illustration: When the artist makes a statue of wood or stone, he does not put the image in the wood; he chips away the wood which hides the form. He gives the wood nothing, he takes it away: carves it out where too thick, pares off overlay, and then there appears what was hidden. This is the treasure hid in a field, of which our Lord tells in the Gospel.

Saint Augustine says that when the human soul is all upturned into eternity, into God and God alone, then God's image lightens and shines; but when the soul faces outward, even in good outward works, then the image is veiled. That is what is meant by the women's heads being covered while the men's are bare, in Saint Paul's teaching. And in all downward turning of the soul, what it is turning to means the same thing: a covering, a head cloth. But the upturned face of the soul is God's bare form, God's birth, naked, unveiled in the naked soul of the noble man as God's image, God's Son, the seed of divine nature in us which never dies out, though by chance covered over. As David says in the Psalms: Though suffering and sorrow are man's portion yet shall he abide in the image of God and that image in him. The true light shines in the darkness, but we are not aware of it.

In the Song of Songs it is written: Look not upon me because I am brown, for I am shapely and beautiful, only the sun has altered my color. The sun is the light of this world, so it means that the highest and best things created or made will dim and discolor the divine image in us. Solomon says: Remove the dross from the silver and there shines forth that purest of vessels, the image of God in the soul.

This too is what our Lord meant when he said, "a nobleman went out." For man has to go out of all forms and of himself, and to all such he must be wholly foreign and remote if he really means and is to be a son; to become the Son in his Father's heart. Means of all kinds are alien to God.

God says, "I am the first and the last." No difference exists either in the nature of God or in the Persons, so far as they are one in nature. The divine nature is one, and each of the Persons also is one, the same one as their nature. Distinction in being and existence is taken as *same* and is one. Where it is not in

God it takes on and has and shows difference. In one, God is found; so to find God a man must be one. Our Lord says: "A man went out." In difference (separation) we find neither one nor reality, nor God nor rest nor bliss nor satisfaction. Be one, that you may find God! And truly, if you were really one, you would stay one in separation, and separation would be one to you, so nothing could stand in your way. One remains equal to one in a thousand thousand stones just as much as it does in four stones, and a million is a simple number just as much as four.

A heathen philosopher says, "The one is gotten of the supreme God. Its idiosyncrasy consists in being one with one. He deceives himself who seeks it under God." And the same philosopher says too that with nothing has this one a truer friendship than with maidens, virgins; as Saint Paul says: "I have espoused you chaste virgins to the one." And so shall mankind be united together to the one, which is God and God only.

"A man went forth," our Lord says. The fundamental meaning of the Latin word for man is, according to one interpretation, a person who submits himself wholly to God with all he is and all that is his, one who looks up to God disregarding his own which he knows is behind him, beneath him. This is perfect and genuine humility. He takes this name from the earth. I will say no more of this now. But this word *man* also means something superior to nature, above time, above temporal things, things smacking of time, place, or body. Further, this man has in one way got nothing in common with nothing, for he is not copied from this or from that, nor is he like them, and he knows nothing of nothing; there is no feeling, no sense of nothingness in him. He is quite free from nothingness. There is found in him only pure being, goodness, and truth. A man of this sort is a noble man and none else. There is yet another way of explaining the term *nobleman* which our Lord uses.

You must know that those who see God face to face see also creatures with him. Intuition is the light of the soul, and all men by nature desire this knowledge. No better thing exists. Intuition is good. Philosophers declare that when we know creatures in themselves, that is evening knowledge, and in this creatures are seen in all sorts of different forms. But when we know creatures in God, that is called morning knowledge, and then creatures are seen all the same, free from form, deprived of all likeness, in the one, God himself. Such is the noble man of whom our Lord says, "A nobleman went out." Noble because he is one and also because he knows God and creatures in one. I will offer still another explanation of what is meant by a nobleman. I say:

When anyone—his soul, his spirit—is contemplating God, then too he is aware and knows that he is seeing; he knows that he is knowing and seeing God. Now there are some who think, and it is quite credible, that the kernel, the flower of felicity, consists in knowing, in the spirit knowing that it is knowing God. For though I had all bliss, yet if I knew it not, what help, what good, would it be to me? But I, of course, would not subscribe to this. For granting that the soul would not be happy without it, nevertheless her happiness does not consist therein, for the first condition of bliss is the vision of God face to face; that is her life and her being. She draws all she is from the ground of God, all unwitting of knowing, unwitting of loving, not knowing of things at all. She is fast asleep in the essence of God, conscious only of being there and of God. If she knows and knows that she knows and sees and loves God, that involves sallying forth, going back to the first in order of nature. To know oneself white is much more external than to be white.

Philosophers say it is one thing, the power whereby the eye sees, and another whereby it knows that it sees. The first, its seeing, all depends on the color, not on the thing colored. It is all one what is colored, stone, wood, man, or angel; to have color, that is the whole thing. Even so, I say that the noble man is drawing, getting his whole being, life, and happiness out of God, in God, and from God alone, not from knowing, seeing, or loving God or anything of that kind. Our Lord said well, it is eternal life simply to know God, the one true God—not to know that one knows God. How should a man know himself God-knowing when he does not even know himself? Surely, though, a man does not know himself, he knows God alone and nothing else at all, when he goes to heaven and is happy in the root and ground of happiness. But when the soul knows she knows God, then she knows God and herself as well. As I was saying just now, it is one thing, the power whereby a man sees, and another the power whereby he knows and is aware that he sees. As a matter of fact, now, here in us, the power whereby we see and know that we see is nobler and higher than the power by which we see, for nature begins its work with the weakest, but God starts his work with the strongest, most forward. Nature makes the man from the child and the hen from the egg, but God makes the man before the child and the hen before the egg. God gives the Holy Ghost before he gives the gifts of the Holy Ghost.

My verdict then is this: Though man may know and realize that he is seeing and knowing God, his happiness does not depend on this, nor would God wish my happiness to lie therein. He who would have it otherwise must settle it with himself—I am sorry but I cannot help it. Heat of the fire and the nature of fire are totally different things and poles apart in nature, albeit near allied in time and place.

God's seeing and my seeing are poles apart and quite unlike each other. Well indeed may our Lord say a nobleman went out into a far country to receive a kingdom, and returned. For man must be one in himself, he must seek for that in himself and in one and "receive" in one: see God and God only. And returning means recognition: seeing and knowing that he sees and knows God.

All this the prophet Ezekiel has already said where he speaks of a great eagle with great wings, long-limbed, full of feathers and of variety, coming to the pure mountain and taking away the pith or marrow of the highest tree and cropping off the topmost branch which he brought down. What our Lord calls a nobleman Ezekiel describes as a great eagle. Who is nobler than he who is begotten half of the highest and best that creature has and the other half of the innermost ground of the divine nature, of its solitariness?

In the prophet Hosea our Lord says: "I will lead the noble souls into the desert and will speak to their hearts," one to one, one from one, one in one and in one one eternally.

On Detachment

I have read many works of both heathen masters and prophets, and books of the Old and New Testaments, and have sought earnestly and with the utmost diligence to find out what is the best and highest virtue, with the aid of which man could be most closely united with God, by which man could become by grace what God is by nature, and by which man would be most like the image of what he was when he was in God, when there was no difference between him and God, before God had created the world.

And when I search the Scriptures thoroughly, as far as my reason can fathom and know, I just find that pure detachment stands above all things, for all virtues pay some regard to the creatures, yet detachment is free from all creatures. Hence it was that our Lord said to Martha: "One thing is needful," that is to say, he who wishes to be untroubled and pure must have one thing, namely detachment.

The teachers praise love most highly, as Saint Paul does when he says: "In whatever tribulation I may find myself, if I have not love, I am nothing." But I praise detachment more than all love. First, because the best thing about love is that it forces me to love God. On the other hand, detachment forces God to love me. Now it is much nobler that I should force God to myself than that I should force myself to God.

And the reason is that God can join himself to me more closely and unite himself with me better than I could unite myself with God. That detachment forces God to me I can prove by the fact that everything likes to be in its own natural place. Now God's own and natural place is unity and purity, and they come from detachment. Hence God must of necessity give himself to a detached heart.

Secondly, I praise detachment more than love because love forces me to suffer all things for the sake of God, but detachment makes me receptive of nothing but God. Now it is far nobler to be receptive of nothing but God than to suffer all things for the sake of God. For in suffering man pays some attention to the creatures through which he has the suffering. On the other hand, detachment is completely free from all creatures. That detachment is receptive of nothing but God I prove by the fact that whatever is to be received must be received in something or other. Now detachment is so near nothingness that nothing is so delicate that it could remain in detachment except God alone. He is so simple and delicate that he can be quite well contained in the detached heart. Therefore detachment is receptive of nothing but God.

The masters also praise humility above many

other virtues. But I praise detachment above all humility, and for this reason: humility can exist without detachment, but perfect detachment cannot subsist without perfect humility. For perfect humility tends to its own destruction; but detachment borders so closely on nothing that between perfect detachment and nothingness there can be nothing. Therefore perfect detachment cannot exist without humility. Now two virtues are always better than one.

The second reason why I praise detachment more than humility is that perfect humility bows down beneath all creatures, and in this bending down man goes out of himself and into the creatures. But detachment remains within itself. Now no going out can ever be so noble as the indwelling is in itself. Therefore the prophet said: "Omnia gloria eius filiae regis ab intus"; that is to say, "The king's daughter has all her glory from her inwardness." Perfect detachment is not in the least inclined to bow down beneath any creature or above any creature. It wishes to be neither below nor above; it wishes to stand by itself, giving neither joy nor sorrow to anyone, and wishing to have neither equality nor inequality with any creature, desiring neither this nor that. It does not wish for anything but to exist. To be either this or that is not its wish. For if anyone wishes to be this or that, he wants to be something, but detachment wishes to be nothing. For this reason it is not a burden to anything.

Now one might say that all virtues were present in our Lady to perfection, and therefore she must also have possessed perfect detachment. If, then, detachment is higher than humility, why did our Lady pride herself on her humility and not on her detachment, when she said, "Quia respexit dominus humilitatem ancillae suae," that is to say, "He regarded the humility of his handmaiden." Why did she not say, "He regarded the detachment of his handmaiden"? To this I reply that in God there are both detachment and humility, so far as we can speak of virtue in God. Now you should know that it was his loving humility that led God to deign to assume human nature. His detachment stood immovable in itself when he became man, just as it had done when he created heaven and earth, as I shall explain to you shortly. And since our Lord, when he was about to become man, remained immovable as regards his detachment, our Lady knew full well that he also expected the same of her, and that in this matter he considered her humility and not her detachment. Therefore she stood immovable in her detachment, and she prided herself on her humility, not on her detachment. And if she had only

110

said one word about her detachment, such as "He regarded my detachment," then the detachment would have been marred and it would not have been entire and perfect, for then she would have gone out of herself. There can be no departure from detachment, however small, which leaves detachment unblemished. And thus you have the reason why our Lady prided herself on her humility and not on her detachment. Hence the prophet said, "Audiam, quid loquatur in me dominus meus"; that is to say, "I will be silent and will hear what the Lord my God will say in me," as if he were to say, "If God wishes to speak to me, let him enter, I will not go out."

I also praise detachment more than all mercy, for mercy simply means that man, going out of himself, turns to the failings of his fellow men and for this reason his heart is troubled. Detachment is free from this; it remains in itself and does not allow itself to be troubled by anything, because, as long as anything can trouble a man, it is not well with him. In short, if I consider all virtues, I find that none is so completely without defects and so applicable to God as is detachment.

There is a master named Avicenna, who says: "The nobility of the soul that is detached is so great that whatever it looks upon is true, and whatever it asks for is granted, and whatever it orders must be obeyed." And you should know as a fact that whenever the free spirit is to be found in true detachment, it forces God to its being. If it could exist in a formless state and without any accidents, then it would receive God's properties in itself. But God cannot give that to anyone but himself; hence God cannot do anything more for the detached spirit than to give himself to it. And the man who thus stands in complete detachment is rapt into eternity in such a way that no transient thing can move him and he feels nothing at all that is physical. He is said to be dead to the world, for nothing that is worldly tastes good to him. This is what Saint Paul had in mind when he said, "I live and yet not I, but Christ lives in me."

Now you might ask, what is detachment, since it is so noble in itself? Here you should know that true detachment is nothing other than this: the spirit stands as immovable in all the assaults of joy or sorrow, honor, disgrace or shame, as a mountain of lead stands immovable against a small wind. This immovable detachment brings about in man the greatest similarity with God. For if God is God, he has it from his immovable detachment, and from this detachment he has his purity, his simplicity, and his immutability. And therefore, if man is to become like God, as far as a creature can possess similarity to God, it must be by means of detachment. It is this that leads man to purity and from purity to simplicity and from simplicity to immutability. And these things bring about a certain similarity between God and man. But this similarity must take place through grace, for grace draws man away from all temporal things and purifies him from all transient things.

It is right that you should know that to be empty of all creatures is to be full of God, and to be full of all creatures is to be empty of God. You should also know that in this immovable detachment God has dwelt eternally and he still dwells in it. And you should know that when God created heaven and earth and all creatures, that affected his immovable detachment as little as if the creatures had never been created. Indeed, I will say more: all the prayers and all the good works which man can perform in the world have as little effect on God's detachment as if neither prayers nor good works had ever been carried out. On that account God will not be any milder or more favorably inclined to mankind than if the prayers or good works had never been performed. Indeed, I will go further: when the Son in the Deity wished to become man, and did so, and suffered his passion, that affected the immovable detachment of God as little as if he had never become man.

Now you might say, "That means that all prayers and all good works are lost, because God does not undertake to be moved by anyone by these means. Yet it is said that God wishes to be asked for everything." Here you should pay careful attention and rightly understand, if you can, that God in his first eternal glance, if we could assume that there was one, considered all things to see how they were to take place, and saw in this glance when and how he was to create the creatures and when the Son was to become man and suffer. He also saw the smallest prayer and good work that anyone was destined to perform, and he considered what prayer and devotion he was to answer. He saw that you will urgently call upon him tomorrow and earnestly pray, and God will not answer the call and prayer tomorrow, for he has already answered it in his eternity before you ever became man. But if your prayer is not wholehearted and is not sincere, God will not refuse you now, for he has refused you already in his eternity.

Thus, in his first eternal glance God has considered all things, and God performs nothing anew, since it has all been decided beforehand. And so God dwells always in his immovable detachment; and yet for this reason the prayers and good works of people are not lost. For if anyone does well, he will be well rewarded, and he who does evil will also be rewarded accordingly. Saint Augustine says the same thing in the fifth book of *De Trinitate,* in the last chapter: "God forbid that anyone should say that God loved anyone in time, for with him nothing has passed away and also nothing is future, and he loved all the saints before the world was made, as he foresaw. When it happens that he makes manifest in time what he foresaw in eternity, people think that God has acquired a new love. And in the same way, when he is angry or does a kind action, it is we who are changed, whereas he remains unchangeable, just as the sun's rays hurt weak eyes and do good to healthy ones, although the sun's rays remain unchangeable in themselves." Similarly, Augustine says in the twelfth book of *De Trinitate,* in the fourth chapter, "God does not see in a temporal manner and no new sight arises in him."

In this sense also Isidore speaks in his book *Of the Highest Good* as follows: "Many people ask what God was doing before he created heaven and earth, or from whence came the new intention in God to make the creatures. And I answer thus: No new intention ever arose in God, for although the creature did not exist in itself as it is now, it was from eternity in God and in his reason." God did not create heaven and earth as we say they were made in our worldly fashion, for all creatures were spoken in the eternal Word. Moreover, we can also quote the words which the Lord spoke to Moses when Moses said to the Lord: "Lord, if Pharaoh says to me, Who are you, how am I to answer him?" Then the Lord said: "Then say I am that I am has sent you." That means, he who is immutable in himself, he has sent me.

Now one might say: "Had Christ also this unchangeable detachment when he said: "My soul is sorrowful even unto death," and Mary, when she stood beneath the Cross? And yet much has been said about her lamentations. How can all this be reconciled with immovable detachment? In this connection you should know that the masters tell us that in every man there are two kinds of men. The first is called the outward man, that is, sensitivity. This man is served by the five senses and yet the outer man operates by the power of the soul. The second man is called the inward man: that is the inmost part of the man. Now you should know that a religious man who loves God uses the powers of the soul in the outward man no further than what the five senses require as a matter of necessity. And the inward man does not heed the five senses, except insofar as he is their guide and leader. He takes care that they do not apply themselves to their object in a bestial manner, as some people do who live according to the lusts of the flesh, like the beasts which are without reason. Such people are more properly described as animals than as human beings.

Whatever powers the soul has left over from what she gives to the five senses, the soul gives these powers entirely to the inward man, and when he has any high and noble object in view, the soul draws to herself all the powers which she has lent to the five senses. This man is then called senseless and crazy, for his object is an intellectual image or something transcending reason without an image. Know then that God expects every religious man to love him with all the powers of his soul. Hence he said: "Love your God with all your heart." Now there are some men who completely dissipate the powers of the soul in the outward man. These are the people who direct all their aims and intelligence towards transient possessions, and who know nothing of the inward man.

Now you should know that the outward man may be undergoing trials, although the inward man is quite free from them and immovable. Even in Christ there was an outward man and an inward man, and also in our Lady. Whatever Christ and our Lady ever said of outward things was spoken by the outer man, and the inner man dwelt in immovable detachment. It was thus that Christ said: "My heart is sorrowful even unto death." And however much our Lady lamented and whatever other things she said, she was always in her inmost heart in immovable detachment. Let us take an analogy of this. A door opens and shuts on a hinge. Now if I compare the outer boards of the door with the outward man, I can compare the hinge with the inward man. When the door opens or closes, the outer boards move to and fro, but the hinge remains immovable in one place and it is not changed at all as a result. So it is also here, if you only know how to act rightly.

Now I ask: What is the object of pure detachment? I answer that neither this nor that is the object of pure detachment. It aims at a mere nothing and I will tell you why: pure detachment aims at the highest goal in which God can work entirely according to his will. But God cannot work in all hearts absolutely according to his will. For, in spite of the fact that God is almighty, he cannot work unless he finds readiness or creates it. And I say "creates it," because of Saint Paul, since God found no readiness in him, but he prepared him by means of the inpouring of grace. It is for this reason that I say that God works according as he finds readiness in us. His operation is different in men and in stones; we find a parable of this in nature. If one heats an oven and puts in it a piece of dough made of oats and one of barley and one of rye and one of wheat, there is only one heat in the oven and yet it does not work equally in all the pieces of dough. For one of them turns into a fine loaf, the second is rougher, and the third is rougher still. The heat is not to blame for this, but the material, which is unequal. In the same way, God does not work alike in all hearts, but according as he finds readiness and receptivity. If in some heart there is this or that, there may be something in the "this" or "that" as a result of which God cannot work unhampered.

Hence, if the heart is to find preparedness for the highest of all flights, it must aim at a pure nothing, and in this there is the greatest possibility that can exist. For when the detached heart has the highest aim, it must be toward the Nothing, because in this there is the greatest receptivity. Take a parable from nature: if I want to write on a wax tablet, then no matter how noble the thing is that is written on the tablet, I am nonetheless vexed because I cannot write on it. If I really want to write I must delete everything that is written on the tablet, and the tablet is never so suitable for writing as when absolutely nothing is written on it. In the same way, when God wishes to write on my heart in the most sublime manner, everything must come out of my heart that can be called "this" or "that"; thus it is with the detached heart. Then God can work in the most sublime manner and according to his highest will. Hence the object of the detached heart is neither this nor that.

But now I ask: What is the prayer of the detached heart? I answer that detachment and purity cannot pray. For if anyone prays, he asks God that something may be given to him, or asks that God may take something away from him. But the detached heart does not ask for anything at all, nor has it anything at all that it would like to be rid of. Therefore it is free from all prayer, and its prayer is nothing else than to be uniform with God. On this alone the prayer of detachment rests.

In this sense we may understand what was said by Saint Dionysius on the words of Saint Paul: "There are many of you who all run for a crown, and yet only one can win it." All the powers of the soul run toward the crown, and yet only one being can obtain it. Dionysius says in this connection: "The race is nothing but a turning away from the creatures and unification with uncreatedness." When the soul comes to this, she loses her name and God draws her into himself, so that she becomes nothing in herself, as the sun draws the dawn into itself, so that it is annihilated. Nothing brings man to this but pure detachment. Here we may cite the words of Augustine: "The soul has a heavenly entrance into the Divine nature in which all things become nothing to her." On earth this entrance is simply pure detachment. When the detachment reaches its highest perfection, it becomes unknowing through knowledge, loveless through love, and dark through light.

Hence we may also quote the words of a master: "The poor in spirit are those who have surrendered all things to God, as he had them when we did not exist." No one can do this but a pure detached heart. That God prefers to be in a detached heart rather than in any other is clear, for if you ask me: What does God seek in all things? I should answer in the words of the Book of Wisdom, where he says: "In all things I seek rest." There is nowhere complete rest except in the detached heart alone. For this reason God would rather be there than in any other things or virtues.

You should also know that the more man strives to be receptive of the Divine inflowing, the happier he is, and whoever can place himself in the highest preparedness for it also dwells in the highest happiness. Now no man can make himself receptive of the Divine inflowing except by uniformity with God. For according as every man is uniform with God, he is to that extent receptive of the Divine inflowing. Now uniformity comes from the submission of man to God; in the same measure as man submits himself to the creatures, the less he is uniform with God. Now the pure detached heart is free from all creatures, hence it is entirely subject to God and stands in the greatest possible uniformity with God and it is also most receptive of the Divine inflowing. This is the meaning of Saint Paul's words, "Put on Jesus Christ," and he meant "uniformity with Christ," for the putting on can only take place through uniformity with Christ.

You must know that when Christ became man, he did not become an individual man, but he adopted human nature. Therefore empty yourself of all things in such a way that there only remains what Christ adopted, and in this way you will have put on Christ. If anyone wishes to recognize the nobility and value of perfect detachment, let him take notice of the words of Christ, speaking of his humanity to his disciples: "It is expedient for you that I go away from you, for if I go not away, the Holy Spirit cannot come to you." It was just as if he had said: "You have taken

too much joy in my physical presence, hence the perfect joy of the Holy Spirit cannot be imparted to
you." Therefore strip yourselves of the images and
unite yourselves with the formless Being, for God's
spiritual consolation is gentle. Therefore he will only
offer himself to those who despise bodily comfort.

Now all thoughtful people should take note. No
one is more cheerful than the one who lives in the
greatest detachment. There can never be any physical
or fleshly joy without spiritual loss, for the flesh lusts
against the spirit and the spirit against the flesh.
Therefore, if anyone sows in the flesh inordinate love,
he reaps eternal death, and if anyone sows in the spirit
orderly love, he will reap of the spirit eternal life.
Hence, the more quickly man flees from the creatures, the more quickly the Creator hastens toward
him. All thoughtful persons should take note of this:
although the joy that we might have in the physical
presence of Christ is an obstacle to us in the reception
of the Holy Spirit, how much more detrimental in
our search for God is the inordinate joy which we
have in transient comfort. Therefore, detachment is
the very best thing. It purifies the soul, cleanses the
conscience, inflames the heart, arouses the spirit,
quickens desire, and makes God known. It separates
off the creatures and unites the soul with God. Now

take note, all thoughtful creatures: the swiftest animal that bears you to perfection is suffering, for no one will enjoy more eternal bliss than those who stand with Christ in the greatest bitterness. Suffering is bitter as gall, but to have suffered is honey-sweet. Nothing disfigures the body before men so much as suffering, and yet nothing beautifies the soul before God so much as to have suffered. The securest foundation on which this perfection can rest is humility. For while the natural man crawls here in the deepest lowliness, his spirit flies up into the heights of the Godhead, for joy brings sorrow and sorrow brings joy. If anyone wishes to attain perfect detachment, let him strive for perfect humility, then he will come close to the Godhead. May the highest detachment, that is, God himself, assist us to achieve this. Amen.

For Further Reading

Ancelet–Hustache, Jeanne. *Master Eckhart and the Rhineland Mystics*. Translated by Hilda Graf. New York: Harper Torchbooks, 1957.

Backhouse, Halcyon, ed. *The Best of Meister Eckhart*. New York: Crossroad, 1993.

Blakney, Raymond P., trans. *Meister Eckhart: A Modern Translation*. New York: Harper & Row, 1941.

Breakthrough: Meister Eckhart's Creation Spirituality in New Translation. Introduction and commentary by Matthew Fox. Garden City, N.J.: Doubleday, 1980.

Clark, James M., and John V. Skinner, trans. *Meister Eckhart: Selected Treatises and Sermons Translated from Latin and German*. London: Faber & Faber, 1958.

College, Edmund, O.S.A., and Bernard McGinn, trans. *Meister Eckhart: The Essential Sermons, Commentaries, Treatises, and Defense*. New York: Paulist Press, 1981.

Davies, Oliver, trans. *Meister Eckhart: Selected Writings*. London: Penguin, 1994.

Evans, C. de B., trans. *The Works of Meister Eckhart,*

Doctor Ecstaticus. London: John M. Watkins, 1952.

Pfieffer, Franz, trans. *Meister Eckhart*. London: John M. Watkins, 1956.

The Rhineland Mystics: Writings of Meister Eckhart, Johannes Tauler, and Jan von Ruusbroec, and Selections from the Theologica Germanica. New York: Crossroad, 1990.

Tobin, Frank J. *Meister Eckhart: Thought and Language*. Philadelphia: University of Pennsylvania Press, 1986.

Walshe, M. O'C., trans. *Meister Eckhart: Sermons and Treatises*. Shaftesbury: Element Books, 1987.

Sources and Credits

Sayings

1–8: from *Meister Eckhart: A Modern Translation* by Raymond Bernard Blakney. Copyright 1941 by Harper & Brothers; copyright renewed. Reprinted by permission of HarperCollins Publishers, Inc. 9–17: from *Meister Eckhart,* translated by Franz Pfieffer, with some additions by C. de B. Evans (London: John M. Watkins, 1956).

Selections from "Table Talk"

From *The Works of Meister Eckhart, Doctor Ecstaticus,* translated by C. de B. Evans (London: John M. Watkins, 1952).

Selections from "The Book of Divine Consolation"

From *Master Eckhart and the Rhineland Mystics,* by Jeanne Ancelet-Hustache. Translated by Hilda Graf (New York: Harper Torchbooks, 1957).

Sermons

"This Is Meister Eckhart," "Poverty," and excerpt from "Peace": from *Meister Eckhart,* translated by Franz Pfeiffer. Excerpt from "On Luke 14:16": from *Master Eckhart and the Rhineland Mystics.* "The Love of God": from *Meister Eckhart: A Modern Translation* by Ray-

"The Nobleman"

"On Detachment"

Illustrations